CROWNED
with GRACE

A COLLECTION OF MARIAN TITLES AND DEVOTIONS

INTRODUCTION BY

DR. MARK MIRAVALLE, S.T.D., S.T.L.

WRITE *these* **WORDS**

CATHOLICITY · CREATIVITY · COMMUNITY

Cover and page design by Mike Fontecchio, Faith & Family Publications.

Editorial services provided by Mary Beth Giltner, marybethgiltner.com.

For more information, or to order, please visit: crownedwithgrace.com

Paperback ISBN: 978-1-965803-10-3

Printed in the United States of America

CONTENTS

CONTENTS

INTRODUCTION

When St. Bernard of Clairvaux voiced his famous Marian motto, *"De Maria numquam satis,"* that is, "About Mary you can never say enough," he was not being hyperbolic but rather emphatic about the true glories of the Mother of God. While the British analytical philosopher may take exception, St. Bernard's point is that, within the limits of creature hood and an immaculate humanity, the sublime prerogatives of the ever-Virgin Mary simply go on and on in a seemingly endless list of honors and titles. Surely, if St. Bernard, St. Louis de Montfort, St. Maximilian Kolbe, and St. John Paul II were at table together in heaven enjoying a celestial cappuccino, their only mutual regret would not be that they said "too much" about Mary during their earthly sojourn, but that they didn't say more about the celestial Queen they now venerate face to face.

Since it is near impossible to convey the plenitude of Marian attributes, to capture the "full Mary" in human expression, one fruitful method towards this noble goal is to list and expound upon her many traditional titles and devotions. While no single title can capture the essence of the Mother, identifying and articulating her multiform titles helps to reveal the complete tapestry of the Immaculate Mediatrix of each and every grace, hence the great rhyme and reason for *Crowned with Grace.*

Each Marian title historically ascribed to Our Lady refers to a virtue of Mary, a type of Mary, a role of Mary, or devotion to Mary. Since her virtues, quintessentially worthy of our imitation and love, are as numerous as her repeated good acts, this category alone stands without limit. Her types are usually taken from Scripture and indicate a biblical foreshadowing of who the Mother of Jesus would be in perfect service to her Son. Mary's titles often indicate expressions of her actual maternal roles and functions on behalf of her earthly children.

Three Marian titles in particular merit our special attention, for these three titles constitute three critical motherly functions which humanity seriously and existentially needs at our present historical moment.

Mary's title as human "Co-redemptrix"* denotes the unique and unparalleled cooperation of Mary with and under Jesus Christ in the Redemption of humanity. God willed that the same three elements causing the disastrous fall of humanity would be used for its restoration: a man, a woman, and a tree. Hence the role of Mary, the New Eve, at the side of Christ, the New Adam on the tree of Calvary was not accidental, but in fact essential in the Father's plan of Redemption. Mary's role as the ancient New Eve is captured today in the title, Co-redemptrix. She is the "Mother suffering" who joined like no other creature in the sufferings of Jesus for our salvation. She continues her mystical suffering for her children today.

Mary is also the "Mediatrix of all graces."* Each and every grace we receive from Jesus comes through the hands and heart of Mary. Once again, Mary's title as Mediatrix of all graces reveals her function. She mediated Jesus, the source of all grace, to humanity when she said "yes" at the Annunciation. Today, she continues to intercede for every created grace humanity receives from the Heart of her all-merciful Son. She is the "Mother Nourishing."

Mary's most ancient title is "Advocate." She brings the needs of humanity to the throne of Jesus, our King. As Queen and Advocate,

---

* On November 4, 2025, the Vatican Dicastery for the Doctrine of the Faith (DDF) issued a doctrinal note regarding the usage of the Marian titles, "Co-redemptrix" and "Mediatrix of All Graces." The publisher and authors herein agree to profess, protect, and promulgate the Scriptural and Traditional revelation of the infinite primacy of Jesus Christ as our only divine Mediator and Redeemer and further acknowledges the subordinate and unparalleled human participation and cooperation of the Immaculate Virgin Mary, Mother of Jesus Christ, in the historic work of Redemption.

she is the greatest intercessor between Jesus and the human race, forever seeking ways to unite her later children with her First Child. As universal Advocate, She protects, defends, and intercedes, especially in times of danger. She is the "Mother pleading."

Since 1915, an international movement in the Catholic Church has petitioned the various popes to solemnly define Our Lady's role as Spiritual Mother of all peoples, inclusive of her three maternal titles as Co-redemptrix, Mediatrix, and Advocate. Why?

Precisely because Mary's titles are indeed her functions and when the Vicar of Christ solemnly recognized these maternal roles of Mary, then and only then can she fully exercise these powerful roles of maternal love and intercession for the world. God does not permit grace to be forced upon the human race; we must manifest our free consent, our fiat, our "yes" to Our Lady's full intercession for it to be fully activated.

Any peripheral reading of today's headlines and their unprecedented crises bespeak the need, the peaceful urgency, for this solemn proclamation and consequently the full, historic release of grace from the Mediatrix of all graces that our present age so desperately needs.

This is why a new appreciation, a new papal proclamation of these three Marian titles, as well as a renewed overall appreciation of who Mary is, as so beautifully expressed in various ways in all her titles and honors, is so important now, in our present challenging times. The Mother, as thus appointed by the Most Holy Trinity, is our remedy.

Congratulations to the contributors and to the readers of *Crowned with Grace*. May this little work serve as a humble but authentic contribution to the ultimate fulfillment of Scripture that "all generations will call me blessed (Luke 1:48)."

–Dr. Mark Miravalle
St. John Paul II Chair of Mariology, Franciscan University of Steubenville
Constance Shifflin-Blum Chair of Mariology, Ave Maria University
President, International Marian Association

I

CAUSE OF OUR JOY

How Mary Helps Us to Rejoice in All Things

Claire Dwyer

Praise the Lord!
Sing to the Lord a new song,
his praise in the assembly of the faithful.
Let Israel be glad in its Maker;
let the children of Zion rejoice in their King.
Let them praise his name with dancing,
making melody to him with tambourine and lyre.
For the Lord takes pleasure in his people;
he adorns the humble with victory.

—Psalm 149:1–4

As I write this, it is September 9, and just yesterday the Church celebrated Our Lady's Nativity. My kids, as they always do on September 8, sang "Happy Birthday" at school and indulged in trays of cookies. The daily office for the feast of Mary's birth exclaims: "*Your birth, O Virgin Mother of God, proclaims joy to the whole world,* for from you arose the glorious Sun of Justice, Christ our God; he freed us from the age-old curse and filled us with holiness; he destroyed death and gave us eternal life."

Causa nostrae laetitiae, or Cause of Our Joy, is a title of Our Lady that is included in the Litany of Loreto, approved by Pope Sixtus V in 1587. For centuries, the Church has held Mary up as a radiant light casting out the despair and darkness of our lives.

The Church also holds, as she always does, a mysterious tension between two truths.

For the Cause of Our Joy is also Our Lady of Sorrows—a title that is meaningful for me because, while we celebrate Mary's birthday on September 8, I celebrate mine on September 15—the feast of Our Lady of Sorrows.

For a number of years, once I was old enough to realize what this feast was, I felt a little . . . cheated. I mean, it's a bit of a let-down to liturgically commemorate all the bitterness in Mary's life on the day you're supposed to be celebrating your own. Not that I ever thought it should be all about me, but as a child, it just didn't seem quite fair. To enter the world as we stand with Mary at the Cross.

Eventually, I made peace with it. And then later still I considered it an honor to be born on a Marian day, whichever one it may be. Forever I'll be tucked into that title like a baby in a blanket, a little footnote on her calendar. And as I got older, the meaning of suffering, hers and my own, took on its own strange beauty.

Cause of Our Joy and Our Lady of Sorrows: We can hold together these two ancient titles of Mary, each one like a mirror reflecting the other, returning its own light. Each one is meaningless, really, without the other. There is no joyful redemption without the Cross, and no value in suffering without its little Sunday at the end. There just isn't. It's one of those paradoxes our faith is famous for.

So Our Lady of Sorrows comes first, the woman who tasted bitterness at the prophecy of Simeon, when she heard that a sword would pierce her heart, already fear stabbing her. But then, as always, a yes. Each sorrow a yes. Specifically, we remember seven: the prophecy of Simeon; the flight into Egypt; the loss of the child Jesus in the Temple; their meeting on the way to Calvary; Jesus' death on the Cross; Mary's reception of Jesus' body; and the placing of his body in the tomb.

Those are the big sorrows Mary bore, but she endured so many little piercings, too—each step he took away from her into the crowds that would eventually kill him, each soul that rejected him, each sin she saw—each one was an ache. But every time there was the yes, the giving away of herself into the will of God. Every sorrow was sealed with a "fiat" that gave it eternal power. Until finally that fiat would culminate at the foot of the Cross, with her leaning into that will with a silent agony we can only imagine.

And then. In that darkest hour, in the horrible silence as heaven held its breath, He spoke. "Woman, behold your son . . . behold your mother." In that extreme grief, she still offered yet another yes. And we all flooded into her heart, hollowed out as it was by humility and suffering. The day he wrenched eternal life back for us, he gave us the source of his own human life: he handed us his Mother.

And we won twice.

She is the Cause of Our Joy because in another act of generosity only possible for God himself, she is ours. *Our* Lady. In the most anguished hour of all her sorrows, we received a gift that the angels would envy if they could envy. We share her with them as a Queen, but only to us can she be a Mother. In all things she shares our life and loves us with unspeakable tenderness.

Once we have become her children, we feel the warm, gentle weight of her gaze that makes life bearable even in its most difficult days. "Our faith tells us that here below, in our present life, we are pilgrims, wayfarers," says St. Josemaría Escrivá. "Our lot is one of sacrifices, suffering, and privations. Nonetheless, joy must mark the rhythm of our steps. 'Serve the

Lord with joy'—there is no other way to serve him."[1] Every shimmering joy, each a foretaste of the eternal that awaits us, comes from her spoon.

She is also the Cause of Our Joy because, by the design of God, it is only through her that Jesus came. Christ, our salvation, came through this little vessel, and we are forever grateful. From the first, the big *fiat* given at the Annunciation, divinity took flesh within her, and finally our salvation was underway. She is the first chapter in the book of eternal life. Joy itself comes to the world, and only through Mary. St. John the Baptist was the first to feel it, leaping with joy as an unborn baby as he felt their presence, even as she herself exclaimed, "My soul magnifies the Lord, and my spirit rejoices in God my Savior" (Luke 1:47).

Appropriately, then, we rejoice too because she is honored in heaven and on earth. She is given a seat next to her Son, she is crowned Queen of Heaven, the final victory is given to her. "A great portent appeared in heaven: a woman clothed with the sun, with the moon under her feet, and on her head a crown of twelve stars" (Revelation 12:1). If our Mother is Queen, then we take heart. St. Josemaría Escrivá reminds us that we are prompted to "acknowledge the basis for this joyful hope. Yes, we are still pilgrims, but our mother has gone ahead, where she points to the reward of our efforts. She tells us we can make it. And, if we are faithful, we will reach home."[2] So she is the Cause of Our Joy because she is a sign of our salvation. What we hope for she holds high as a promise fulfilled.

Finally—and this is the difficult part, but what brings it all full circle—Our Lady of Sorrows is the Cause of Our Joy because Mary enjoyed the happiness of suffering with Christ, suffering for him, and more than anyone else, suffering as he did. She teaches us what it means to suffer well and to bear it with grace, to unite our crosses with his, and to be grateful for the opportunity to become more like him in all things— even, especially, in the hard ones. If we allow her to be our teacher, to

---

1   St. Josemaría Escrivá, *Christ Is Passing By* (New York: Scepter), originally published as *Es Cristo Que Pasa* (Madrid, 1973), Homily 177.

2   Ibid.

show us what it means to be disciples to the end, we will know joy, even on this earth.

What that means is this: if joy is union with God, then there must be a cross in it for us. No cross, no joy. We can run away from it, and maybe there will be a little relief in the distractions of the world, but we will discover no real joy. Only by leaning in, as she did, can true joy be found. Yet once we do embrace our own crosses, we find that being so close to a God who suffered too takes on a certain sweetness. For there can be no Sunday sunrise without Friday's slow fade, no Queen of Heaven without the Sorrowful Mother.

What I have come to appreciate, and even delight in, is that each September 15 is a "happy" birthday after all, in the most joyful sense of the word. And while my naturally melancholic nature[3] tends to veer more in the glass-half-empty, waiting-for-the-other-shoe-to-drop direction, I have taken up some practices to deepen my participation in the joy of heaven.

First of all, I love the practice of a gratitude journal. By focusing on the graces and gifts of God, I am better able to rejoice in his consolations.

Secondly, I try to take time every day to turn off the stream of podcasts, news, and other digital chatter and press my playlist of praise music. It is like entering the anteroom of heaven, the place of true joy, when we lift our hearts and voices in worship.

Finally, I try to slow down and *enjoy the moment*. When we allow ourselves to be present to the everyday miracles of our lives, we find grace and laughter and love all around us. The enemy will try to steal our happiness and be off like a thief with the joy he can no longer know. We must not let him have his way—and we have a mother who has already crushed his head, and who will see to it that we claim, among our inheritance, a share in her joy.

Mater Dolorosa, Causa nostrae laetitiae, ora pro nobis.

---

3   See Claire Dwyer, "The Four Temperaments," March 16, 2019, https://www.clairedwyer.com/the-four-temperaments/

The integration of spiritual direction and creative discernment shapes **Claire Dwyer's** work with writers. As a certified spiritual director and *Full Focus* Certified Coach, she blends proven goal-setting frameworks with creativity and spirituality to help writers and leaders make progress on the projects that matter most. She carries out this work amidst the demanding—but joyful!— duties of family life. See *clairedwyer.com/work-with-me/*.

II

GATE OF HEAVEN

How Mary Brings Heaven to Us and Draws Us to Heaven

Glenn Dickinson

Hail, Star of the Sea,
Nurturing Mother of God
And yet virgin
Happy gate of heaven.

—Ave Stella Maris

The ancient prayer *"Ave Stella Maris"* calls Mary the gate of heaven. When I first encountered this prayer, I was confused by this title of Our Lady. For we know from the Gospels that Jesus alone is the Way to eternal life: "I am the way, and the truth, and the life. No one comes to the Father except through me" (John 14:6).

It seems, then, that Mary could not be validly called "gate of heaven," because Jesus tells us that he is the Way for us to reach heaven. Yet in reality, Mary is indeed the unique gate of heaven. In reconciling these two profound images, we can come to a deeper appreciation, and a deeper love, for Our Lady.

A common feature of Catholic theology is the "both/and." It is one of the qualities that makes Catholic theology so rich and satisfying. When presented with contrasting principles, ideas, and desires, the Church's Magisterium often teaches us not to choose one and eliminate the other, but to find a larger understanding that encompasses and reconciles both.

One classic example of this way of thinking is the question of whether the active life or the contemplative life is the better way to holiness. Do those who devote themselves primarily to prayer and study fail to follow the Gospel, if they seem to give insufficient attention to the corporal works of mercy? On the other hand, the first and greatest commandment is to love the Lord your God with your whole heart, mind, soul and strength (see Matthew 22:36). This comes even before love of neighbor. So do those who devote themselves primarily to the corporal works of mercy fail to follow the first and greatest commandment?

Thankfully, we are not required to choose between these two principles. The Church Fathers tell us that the Christian life requires due attention to both, and that finding the proper mixture is a question of one's individual vocation and state in life.

A similar wisdom governs our understanding of Mary's role in salvation. We must never lose sight of the fact that Jesus is the sole Mediator between heaven and earth (see 1 Timothy 2:5). But as sole Mediator, Jesus can appoint others to complete the work he begins (see Colossians 1:24). His act of redemption can be sufficient without being exclusive. In the same way, his mediation is singular and unique, without necessarily being exhaustive. Thus we read in the *Catechism*:

> "Mary's function as mother of men in no way obscures or diminishes this unique mediation of Christ, but rather shows its power. But the Blessed Virgin's salutary influence on men . . . flows forth from the superabundance of the merits of Christ, rests on his mediation, depends entirely on it, and draws all its power from it." "No creature could ever be counted along with the Incarnate Word and Redeemer; but just as the priesthood of Christ is shared in various ways both by his ministers and the faithful, and as the one goodness of God is radiated in different ways among his creatures, so also the unique mediation

of the Redeemer does not exclude but rather gives rise to a manifold cooperation which is but a sharing in this one source." (CCC 970)

We know this is true through our own experience. Anyone who has ever prayed for another has accepted the role of a kind of mediator and intercessor between that person and God. Yet nothing about this diminishes Our Lord's authority as King of the universe. He is a good king, and he appoints ministers to act on his behalf, with an authority that derives solely from him. To be a faithful Christian means to accept the place in the Kingdom assigned to us and to faithfully carry out our duties.

No Christian in history did this or ever will do this as completely as the Blessed Virgin Mary. We can truthfully say that she was the first Christian. Being the first to do something does not always mean being the best at it, but in this case, it does, for we know that in order to prepare her to be the mother of the incarnate Word, Mary was conceived without sin. By the grace of God, she is the perfect model of how we are meant to respond to God.

Our understanding of Mary is directly related to our understanding of who Christ is. If we recognize who Jesus Christ is, then we must venerate Mary above all other people, indeed, above everything else in all of creation.

As wonderful and awe-inspiring as this is, she is yet still more. And now we come back to the title of this reflection: Mary, Gate of Heaven. Yes, we enter the Kingdom of God through Jesus, but the Kingdom of God first comes to us through Mary. She was the gate by which Jesus the Savior entered our human life in the Incarnation. And because God does nothing in pieces and half measures, she continues to serve as the gate through which Jesus, salvation, and indeed all graces come to us.

Mary provides the way, in her very person, by which Jesus the Redeemer comes into the created world. But this is not the only divine manifestation she embodies. She also is the way by which the Holy Spirit acts in creation.

And the action of the Spirit is not over and done after she conceives Jesus. Again, God does nothing in pieces and half measures. The Holy Spirit continues to act in and through Mary. As St. Maximilian Kolbe wrote, "Mary, as Mother of Jesus our Savior, was made Co-redemptrix of the human race; as the spouse of the Holy Spirit she shares in the distribution of all graces."[1]

The Church has long recognized this title as appropriate to Our Lady's profound contribution to the liberation of all humanity from sin, accomplished by Jesus, which is what we mean by *redemption*. But we must not fall into confusion about this:

> What does "Co-redemptrix" *not* mean in the teachings of the Catholic Church? It does not mean that Mary is a goddess, that she is the fourth person of the Trinity, that she in any way possesses a divine nature, that she is in any fashion not a creature completely dependent upon her Creator like all other creatures. . . .
>
> *Any concept of Mary Co-redemptrix, therefore, that suggests the Mother of Jesus is a fourth Trinitarian person or some type of goddess must be immediately and entirely rejected as grave heresy against Christian revelation. . . .*
>
> *[T]he title "Mary Co-redemptrix" as used by the Church denotes the unique and active participation by Mary, the Mother of Jesus, in the work of Redemption as accomplished by Jesus Christ, the divine and human Redeemer.*[2]

Our Lady's unique status does not raise her beyond her purely human nature, the same nature in all of us. At the same time, she truly stands at the pinnacle of all created beings, higher even than the angels, who recognize her as their queen.

---

1   Manteau-Bonamy, OP, H.M., *Immaculate Conception and the Holy Spirit: The Marian Teachings of St. Maximilian Kolbe* (Libertyville, IL: Marytown Press, 2001), 91.

2   Mark Miravalle, *"With Jesus": The Story of Mary Co-Redemptrix* (Goleta, CA: Queenship Publishing, 2003), 7–8, 9 (emphasis in original).

When we let these realities really sink in, however, we can find ourselves wanting to keep Mary at a distance, precisely because of her holiness and purity. That was certainly my biggest problem, for most of my life. How could I, being the sinner that I am, dare to approach the sinless Mother of God? Wouldn't my sorry condition be a stain on her heavenly beauty?

This reluctance was peeled away in layers, as I grew in understanding of just who she is. The obligations of faith cannot be satisfied merely by learning things, of course. But sometimes a new understanding can open up a new path to relationship. Mary as Gate of Heaven is, for me, that kind of knowledge.

Through her, I saw that heaven extends aid, encouragement, consolation, and many other graces to creatures out of love. Mary above all other created things is the principal and perpetual recipient of those graces—not only for herself, but for us all. To be near her is to be near not only the most loving heart ever created, but the singular place in the whole universe where heaven entered—and continues to enter—creation.

Imagine a doctor who could heal anyone who only drew close. Imagine a bank that could enrich anyone who only stepped inside. Imagine a garden that grew more beautiful the farther you walked down its paths.

To approach Our Lady is to draw close to heaven, simply because she allowed—and still allows—heaven to enter our existence through herself. She is the point at which mere creation touches heavenly perfection. And because heaven is perfect in mercy, there is no danger of any harm to us for daring to go so far.

And yet, who are we to dare it? Consider the many approved apparitions of Our Lady. Each of them is so intimate, for she appears to only a few. She seems to favor children or young women, not adult men or adults in general. Sadly, this might be an indictment of us: we adults are not fit to see such beauty directly. We would see it wrongly, in a way that the innocent do not.

Does this mean we should keep our distance or close our eyes? Of course not. It should give us a new appreciation for the depth of love that God has for us, that he gives so much, even to people like ourselves.

So we must not give up hope. We should pray to have eyes worthy to see the beauty of Mary, the heavenly beauty of the woman through whom God himself chose to enter the world he created. O Happy Gate of Heaven, pray for us!

Glenn Dickinson earned undergraduate degrees in philosophy and journalism before becoming a lawyer. He is a member of the Apostoli Viae community and received a master's certificate in spiritual theology through the Avila Institute. He serves on the board of the St. John Paul II Center for Contemplative Culture. He is married with three adult children and lives in Ventura, California. He blogs on the spirituality of St. John of the Cross at *innerwinecellar.com.*

III

Our Lady of Grace

How Mary Teaches Us to Walk in Trust

Amanda Villagómez

Your word is a lamp to my feet and a light to my path.
—Psalm 119:105

"You're going to have to choose before you know for sure," I said.

The deadline was quickly approaching for my daughter to commit to a university. She had a clear first choice. Her heart longed for all the school would provide: beauty, adventure, growth in independence, solid support to nurture the ongoing development of her faith, and an opportunity to run with a team that would cultivate and challenge her as an athlete.

There was only one major catch: we were not at all prepared for out-of-state expenses. The alternative in-state options were much more practical. I had been hoping that by the time the deadline arrived, the pieces would have all clicked into place, but the time had come for her to decide. We only knew for sure that we could make it work at her preferred school for a *single* term.

I walked her through the different options and what the financial implications might mean, including the extra stress that can come from financial uncertainty and the burden of graduating with debt. She remained firm that she wanted to go to her top choice (in her mind *the* choice), despite the inherent added challenges.

"If you really want to go, you can, but you will have to be prepared to pause or pivot at any point along the way," I said. "You will be taking a calculated risk with support. Whether you are able to stay one quarter, a year, or finish your degree there, you will be OK. I can help you navigate however it unfolds."

So she took a leap and locked in her choice. She traded ease, stability, and financial assurances for sacrifice and uncertainty, knowing she would need to work and take out loans. She was taking a chance with the hope that it would all be worth it.

Ten years ago, I would not have been able to cultivate space for that option to flourish. Instead, I would have wanted to have it all figured out in order to even encourage her to consider choosing that school. Yet, over the span of a decade, I had been invited into deeper trust, with consecration to Jesus through Mary as a key part of that journey.

It all began when copies of Fr. Michael Gaitley's *33 Days to Morning Glory* were offered as gifts throughout my diocese on Ash Wednesday with the intent to lead up to consecration on the Solemnity of the Annunciation. It is probably not a coincidence that I continually find myself drawn to meditate on the first joyful mystery of the Rosary—the moment when Mary courageously gave her wholehearted, free-will fiat without knowing all the details and without knowing for sure how it would all work out. Not only that, meditating on the other mysteries of the Rosary reveals how she continued to say yes amidst the joys, the sorrows, and the unexpected twists and turns of life. As I have pondered her story and mine through the lens of the mysteries of the Rosary, Mary has taught me to give my fiat—*and keep giving it*.

The moment of the Annunciation reveals the source of Mary's strength, courage, and virtue. We even repeat it fifty-three times while praying the Rosary; "Hail Mary, *full of grace*" echoes the Angel Gabriel's greeting at the Annunciation, when he conveyed the Lord's invitation for Mary to be the mother of his Son (Luke 1:28). Mary is full of grace—truly Our Lady of Grace.

Though there are different representations of this particular title of Mary, the one I am most drawn to depicts Our Lady dressed in white with a blue mantle, tenderly gazing downward with her arms outstretched. Combined, the different details capture her simplicity, patience, peace, humility, and receptivity. She shows us how to deeply receive grace and then allow it to flow outwards, expressed through our unique and unrepeatable stories.

God's grace aided Mary as the different circumstances of her life unfolded, even the most unimaginable moments of agony. At the pinnacle of her suffering, as she stood at the foot of the Cross, Jesus gave her and her maternal care to us, conveyed through his words to Saint John: "Here is your mother" (John 19:27). The grace that filled her was meant to be shared—a gift for her *and a gift for us.*

In *Lumen Gentium*, the Church explains Mary's unique role in dispensing graces to us:

> This maternity of Mary in the order of grace began with the consent which she gave in faith at the Annunciation and which she sustained without wavering beneath the cross, and lasts until the eternal fulfillment of all the elect. Taken up to heaven she did not lay aside this salvific duty, but by her constant intercession continued to bring us the gifts of eternal salvation. By her maternal charity, she cares for the brethren of her Son, who still journey on earth surrounded by dangers and cultics, until they are led into the happiness of their true home. Therefore the Blessed Virgin is invoked by the Church under the titles of Advocate, Auxiliatrix, Adjutrix, and Mediatrix. This, however, is to be so understood that it neither takes away from nor adds anything to the dignity and efficaciousness of Christ the one Mediator.[1]

---

1   Second Vatican Council, *Dogmatic Constitution on the Church* (*Lumen Gentium*) (November 21, 1964) §62, https://www.vatican.va/archive/hist_councils/ii_vatican_council/documents/vat-ii_const_19641121_lumen-gentium_en.html.

St. Louis de Montfort also beautifully explains how Mary shares God's grace with us:

> God the Son imparted to his mother all that he gained by his life and death, namely, his infinite merits and his eminent virtues. He made her the treasurer of all his Father had given him as heritage. Through her he applies his merits to his members and through her he transmits his virtues and distributes his graces. She is his mystical channel, his aqueduct, through which he causes his mercies to flow gently and abundantly.[2]

We see Mary's longing to fulfill this role in her apparition to St. Catherine Labouré in 1830, which resulted in the creation of the Miraculous Medal. Mary explained to St. Catherine, "These rays symbolize the graces I shed upon those who ask for them. The gems from which rays do not fall are the graces for which souls forget to ask."[3] Mary wants to be with us as we learn to pray and deepen our intimacy with her Son. She wants to walk with us through our challenges, and she wants to experience our joys alongside us. She loves the role she has been given and is always ready to wrap us in her mantle and stand with us at the foot of our own crosses. She encourages us to step into the adventures of our life with trust.

The weekend we dropped my daughter off at college, her cross country team was running a relay around a lake in the community where the university is located. While waiting for the race to begin, I walked on the trails, taking pictures and documenting the moment. I pondered all that I held in my heart—excitement for my daughter to begin this chapter of her journey, the ache of grief from knowing she would not be coming home with us, and the lingering financial uncertainty of it all.

---

2   St. Louis Marie de Montfort, *True Devotion to the Blessed Virgin* (Montfort Missionaries, 2002), 4, https://www.montfort.org/content/uploads/pdf/PDF_EN_26_1.pdf.

3   Fr. Joseph Dirvin, "Saint Catherine Laboure of the Miraculous Medal," EWTN, https://www.ewtn.com/catholicism/library/saint-catherine-laboure-of-the-miraculous-medal-5307.

As I breathed in the stillness of the lake, the trees, and the mountains, I thought, *I don't know how this will unfold, but I know she will be surrounded with beauty.* The sense of peace when immersed in nature reveals a deeper truth: there is no way to know the details of our future, but we have the assurance of God's goodness. Our hearts long for adventure. Yet sometimes we forget that adventures are more than just excitement. They also necessitate courage, endurance, and hope to navigate all that is required of us through the process.

When we encounter challenging moments that make it difficult to see the beauty, we can draw near to the hearts of the Holy Family and meditate on the mysteries of the Rosary. We can ask Mary to teach us how to live with "thy will be done" hearts—hearts that give resounding fiats rooted in his love as the solid foundation, hearts that are willing to take risks with trust in God's provision, hearts that are willing to keep saying yes as the journey progresses. Through the rhythm of the decades, she teaches us. She shows us how to receive his grace and have the courage to keep going, one bead at a time.

Each of us will face different challenges and adventures in our lives. No matter what we may encounter, we can ask Mary to help us ponder in our hearts as she did, and we can lift up everything in prayer, asking her to intercede for us with her mother's love. Here are some questions to take to prayer:

- What are examples of times when you have been called to step out in trust? How did you grow through the process?
- Who has encouraged or supported you through seasons of vulnerability and uncertainty? Which resources have been pivotal?
- How might you increase your reliance on Mary's maternal care and ask for grace to navigate a current circumstance in your life?

Mary, Our Lady of Grace, you have shown us that God's goodness, rather than ideal circumstances, is our firm foundation. Thank you for teaching us through your life that we are not meant to have it all figured out or to have assurances of a smooth journey in order to give our yes. When we are afraid, teach us to be brave. When we are impatient, remind us that the process of growth and healing lasts a lifetime. When we are shocked and confused, help us to cling to hope. Help us to ask for and receive the graces from God that you so desire to bestow upon us. Thank you for your maternal presence and care throughout all the mysteries of our lives.

Amanda Villagómez believes in the value of story—learning from the experiences of others and exploring the themes woven throughout our lives just waiting to be discovered. Through her writing and teaching, Amanda invites you to consider: What is the story of your soul? She would love to support your process of writing and inquiry. Learn more at *amandavillagomez.com*.

IV

Mary, Mother of the Church

A New Title with Ancient Roots

Grace Abruzzo

*I think the most moving fact in the whole history of
mankind is that wherever the Holy Spirit has desired to
renew the face of the earth He has chosen to do so through
communion with some humble little human creature.*[1]

—Caryll Houselander

Years ago, in a season that I can only describe as a springtime of the
soul, when I was growing in the awareness of the presence of God
and the practice of prayer, I experienced an imaginative interior vision
that I did not understand.

I was a young girl and Our Lady was helping me dress. She pulled
two robes from an ancient wooden chest, both beyond beautiful. One
was in a color radiating joy, and the other in a color I associated with
contemplation, depth, and perhaps something somber. Adult-me,
watching the vision unfold, very much wanted to know what each

---

1 Caryll Houselander, *The Reed of God: A New Edition of a Spiritual Classic* (Notre Dame, IN:
Ave Maria Press, 2006), 31.

dress meant, and little-me wanted to know when I would wear them and for what.

But Our Lady said nothing. She simply smiled and led me to a new place.

There it was night. I was older, and I sat among a number of people gathered around a campfire. Our Lady then took my hand and led me some distance away, to a quiet clearing. Silently she gestured to the sky, which was covered with the most beautiful stars I had ever beheld.

I stood gazing at them, enraptured, almost literally—taken up and into something beyond what I could see, into something bigger than myself. I wanted to stay there forever. But Our Lady redirected me, leading me away from the stars and back to the campfire and the crowd.

I remember, more vividly than the vision itself, the temptation to disappointment at being pulled away from the stars, but also Mary's gentle but firm insistence that I rejoin the group at the campfire. I was puzzled at what all this might mean, but at the advice of my spiritual director, I filed it away to be understood only in time.

More recently, I was on pilgrimage, praying in the Basilica of St. John Lateran in Rome. "Lord," I prayed, "Which title of Our Lady should I write about for the book? Please make it clear and undeniable so that I can stop stressing about it!" I turned and nearly bumped into a statue of Mary, Mother of the Church.

I got my clear answer, but it raised another question. Why this title? This is a question not just for me, but for the Church as a whole: Why her, why now?

The title Mary, Mother of the Church has ancient roots in the early Church Fathers, who saw Mary as the New Eve, Mother of All the Living. St. Paul VI first made this title official only in 1964. St. John Paul II put it into the *Catechism*, and in 2018 Pope Francis made it a feast day. The understanding of Mary's role is not new, but the emphasis is—and that merits special attention.

Today, in our world and in our Church, divisions, disagreements, and hostilities show a divided family. More than ever, we need the help of God and his loving mother.

To understand, we must go back to the beginning, when God fashioned Adam from the clay of the earth and said: "It is not good that the man should be alone; I will make him a helper as his partner" (Genesis 2:18). And so while Adam slept, God opened his side, and taking from it a rib, formed woman to be his helper, in Hebrew, *ezer*.

We know the story: the woman entered into dialogue with the devil and allowed herself to be deceived. Doubting God's goodness, she ate the forbidden fruit and offered it to Adam, who also ate. All hell broke loose, literally and figuratively.

Here it is worth pausing to note a remarkable gem hidden in a Hebrew vocabulary lesson. The word *helper* used to describe Eve in Genesis often strikes modern ears as signifying inferiority, indicating a servant or slave. But in Scripture the Hebrew *ezer* more frequently indicates "help" from *more* powerful sources—especially from God himself.[2]

Eve did not "help" in the way God intended. Instead, she "helped" Adam to bring about the fall of the human race. Nor was she passive; she was an active agent in Adam's sin.

Millennia later, at the Annunciation, Mary humbly identified herself as a handmaid or servant. Yet by freely and fully cooperating with the will and plan of God, she became the *ezer* for mankind that God intended.

Mary was the first to receive—and to hold—the Good News. The Church Fathers tell us that Mary conceived Jesus first in her heart and then in her womb. She welcomed, nourished, and gave life to the Word with all she was. She alone never by sin rejected any part of the Word of God. She alone stood in total enmity against the Ancient Serpent, the Father of Lies. She is model and mother of all believers. In her obedience

---

2   Sarah E. Fisher, "Helper: Defining the Ezer Woman," *Hebrew Word Lessons*, May 13, 2018, https://hebrewwordlessons.com/2018/05/13/helper-defining-the-ezer-woman/.

she "untied the knot of Eve's disobedience"; her Yes as the New Eve opened the door to the Yes of Jesus, the New Adam. She became the new "Mother of All the Living"—the Mother of the Church.

We see here highlighted a mystery of God's mercy and magnanimity: the All-Powerful God delights in having human helpers. He doesn't need us (or even Mary). Yet he invites us not only to share his divine nature but also to help his divine work.

In the Gospels we see Mary specifically emerge as the new Eve—the new *ezer* for the New Adam—in two places. In both, we hear echoes of Genesis 3:15, God's promise to put enmity between the serpent and the Woman, as Jesus deliberately addresses his beloved mother as "Woman."

First, at the Wedding in Cana (John 2:1–11), Mary notices that "they have no wine." She sees more than a looming social catastrophe. In bringing this petition to Jesus, Mary seeks not just the temporary joy, the wine, to save this very human wedding banquet. She is petitioning the Bridegroom for the Wine of the Eternal Wedding Feast.

But Mary senses that in asking this, she is offering Jesus a greater invitation: to open his public mission. She knows it will cost—and that she will share that cost. Like the first Eve, she hands to the New Adam an opportunity to choose. But here it is not the forbidden fruit, but the fruit of sacrificial obedience that Mary offers to the New Adam.

And although Jesus at first seems to refuse her ("Woman, what concern is that to you and to me? My hour has not yet come"), she confidently turns to the servants, saying only: "Do whatever he tells you."

We know what follows. The water made into wine of such quality that the steward is rebuked for saving the "best wine for last." Wine of startling abundance—likely between 120 and 180 gallons, more than even the largest wedding might need. We see from Mary's faith that the fruit of obedience is superabundant joy.

But there is always more. Water was turned into wine. Then, at the Last Supper, wine was turned into Blood. And Our Lady stood at the foot of the Cross, receiving this wine—watching as his love and life poured out. Her heart was the chalice shaped to perfectly receive.

And there, at the foot of the Cross, Jesus gave her yet another gift: "Woman, here is your son." And then, "'Son, here is your mother.' From that hour the disciple took her into his own home" (John 19:26–27). Fr. Wilfried Stinissen, O.C.D., writes, "When Pope Paul VI proclaimed Mary Mother of the Church, this was only a confirmation of a reality the Church had been living her entire history, a history that began at the foot of the Cross. When John invited Mary to live with him, it was the Church that acknowledged Mary as her Mother."[3]

Having given us his mother, Jesus yields himself to his Father: "Into your hands I commend my spirit" (Luke 23:46). Shortly afterward, "one of the soldiers pierced his side with a spear, and at once blood and water came out" (John 19:34). In the pierced side of Jesus, the Church Fathers saw the opening from which the Church was born. Just as Eve was taken from Adam's side as he slept, the Church was born from Christ's wounded side as he slept in death. And as the soldier's lance pierced her own heart, Mary our mother experienced the pangs of labor at the birth of her Son's Mystical Body, the Church.

After the crucifixion, there is a certain silence. "On Holy Saturday," John Paul II notes, "the Church, once again, identifies herself with Mary: all her faith is gathered in her, the first believer. In the darkness that envelops creation, she remains alone to keep the flame of faith alive, preparing to welcome the joyful and surprising announcement of the resurrection."[4]

Scripture next shows us Mary with the Church: praying, on the morning of Pentecost, with 120 other followers of Jesus. The same Holy

---

3   Fr. Wilfried Stinissen, O.C.D., *Mary and the Bible in Our Lives*, trans. Sister Claire Marie O.C.D. (San Francisco: Ignatius Press, 2018), 88.

4   Pope John Paul II, General Audience, April 3, 1996, #2, https://www.vatican.va/content/john-paul-ii/it/audiences/1996/documents/hf_jp-ii_aud_19960403.html.

Spirit that overshadowed her at the Annunciation suddenly comes rushing upon them all in the form of wind and fiery tongues.

As they are transformed individually and communally, the first manifestations of the Holy Spirit recall the gift of Cana: "They are filled with new wine" (Acts 2:13). Curious onlookers say it in mockery, but they unwittingly indicate a new reality. It is the joy of the Gospel: Christ's life and work continue in the Church through the Holy Spirit—in each member, and in the Church as a whole.

And it is on the day immediately following Pentecost that Pope Francis situated the new feast day of Mary Mother of the Church. This placement of the feast invites us to see Mary's continued maternal presence and help, as we too are called to become Christ, both individually and communally.

Mary as mother tenderly cares for each of us, guiding and interceding with her spouse, the Holy Spirit, helping to form and fashion us each into the likeness of her Son. And even as we are personally formed, we are simultaneously called to communion; we are not to exist as isolated bodies, but as loving members of Christ's One Body, the Church.

We don't need to look far for evidence that the Body of Christ today is deeply wounded—with scandal, with division, with disobedience and the fruits of sin. Suffering voices from within and without echo Christ's call of thirst from the Cross. Our world is desperate for new wine.

And in this need, we too are invited to obediently accept from Mary a mission for the Church; we too are called to be helpers.

I still do not fully understand the vision from long ago, but nine years ago I stood again looking up at the stars. I had in fact been pulled away from the world I knew—leaving behind my friends, my job, and the life I had built, to return home to care for my mother who was hospitalized with a mysterious illness. I was also caring for my father who was still living, and I spent many days moving from crisis to crisis. In the midst of chaos, I felt isolated and overwhelmed. I would often come home close to midnight and would pause to stare up at the stars. Looking back, I can see the outstretched hand of Our Lady.

This very extended season of care has brought greater aloneness and contemplation but also occasions for sacrifice and self-gift as I seek to love others more concretely. I was brought beyond my own family to be with others who also needed me, and who God knew I needed. Our Lady has been mother and helper to me as she invites me to deeper humility and deeper trust.

"Do whatever he tells you." This wasn't the life I planned or chose. And yet I've begun to taste the wine of Cana, a joy that hints at more that is to come.

Mary, Mother of the Church, help us to be the helpers God desires us to be.

***

Grace Abruzzo is a Catholic writer and speaker on healing, a life of prayer, and God's ever-surprising gifts. Through honest story-telling, humorous reflections, and spiritual insight, she reveals spaces where grace can be found even in life's mess. She currently is a caregiver for her mother, and leads pilgrimages part-time for Syversen Touring. She is the Community Manager for the PraiseWriters community. Visit *graceabruzzo.com*.

V

OUR LADY OF MIRACLES

How Mary Our Mother Works Wonders in Our Lives

Christine Arata

So I tell you, whatever you ask for in prayer, believe
that you have received it, and it will be yours.

—Mark 11:24

It was sometime in the 1980s that I first discovered the Madonna dei Miracoli. The original statue is located in Cicagna, Italy, but my first encounter with Our Lady took place, not in Italy, but in San Francisco at Saints Peter and Paul Church, which houses a painting of the Madonna, or Nostra Signora dei Miracoli, as she is also referred to, and as the patroness of Cicagna.

The image struck me because my great-grandmother, Maria, was from the town of Cicagna. Born in 1872, she surely would have been familiar with the miraculous statue of the Madonna in Cicagna.

The miracle of the Our Lady of Miracles occurred in Cicagna on September 15, 1537, when a well-worn wooden statue of the Madonna was suddenly transformed. Without any natural cause or explanation, it became brightly colored, and the wilted flowers that were on the nearby altar miraculously blossomed. Five witnesses documented this momentous event; it was officially confirmed a miracle.[1]

The painting at Saints Peter and Paul Church in San Francisco is a reproduction of that statue. It portrays the Madonna holding baby Jesus, with St. Dominic on her right and St. Rose of Lima on her left. The inscription on the framed painting reads,

> N.S. DEI MIRACOLI
> VENERATA IN CICAGNA
> CORONATA IL 14 SETTEMBRE 1790
> SAN FRANCISCO 1937

Saints Peter and Paul Church was established to support the influx of Italian immigrants arriving in San Francisco in the late 1800s. Located in the North Beach District, or "Little Italy" as it was called in those early days, the parish became a community for immigrants who felt alone in this new city, far away from the family and traditions they had left behind to come to the United States. My father's grandparents (on both sides of his family) were among the Italian parishioners who found a new home at Saints Peter and Paul. I never knew my great-grandparents, but my grandmother (the daughter of Maria) passed down stories about them. I know the church itself as "the Italian Church" because that's how my family referred to it. This is the church where my grandparents and parents were married, and where my brother and sister (and later, her children and grandchildren) were baptized. By the time I was born, my parents had moved to the other side of town so I was baptized at St. Gabriel's Church in the Sunset District.

The first Mass was celebrated in the church in 1884. Sadly, the first building was destroyed in the San Francisco fire and earthquake in 1906.

---

1   "Sanctuary of Our Lady of Miracles in San Giovanni Battista, Cicagna: A Journey Between Faith and History," Santuari e Miracoli, accessed October 2, 2025, https://www.santuari.eu/en/our-lady-of-miracles-in-san-giovanni-b/.

It was replaced by the current Gothic and Romanesque-style church, which was completed in 1924. As the years went on, the connection between Italy and the San Francisco parish remained strong, with news updates going back and forth. In 1937, there was a celebration of Our Lady of Miracles, along with a new hymn sent from Cicagna. Parishioners prayed a novena for the feast, and they gathered for Mass, a procession, and solemn benediction on September 15. (I like to assume my family members were there, including my father who would have been a teenager then.) The church thought it important to allow its parishioners to practice their regional traditions, which helped boost their spirits, especially during the Great Depression.[2]

The parish celebrated its 100th anniversary in 2024. This in itself is a miracle, when so many other churches have closed and been converted into other types of buildings! I still make it a habit to visit the Madonna dei Miracoli here. Over the years, Mother Mary has repeatedly confirmed my faith that miracles can happen and that she herself continues to intercede for me before Jesus.

I find going to light a candle before the image comforting. I light my candle and then go on with my day. I leave hopeful and trusting that Our Lady will handle whatever situation or need I am facing. Where Mary is, so is Jesus.

While my mom was living, I would ask her for prayers almost daily. For many years, I stopped practicing my faith, but my mother's prayers helped me cope with life, whether I had struggles with relationships, friendships, work, or my health. When my mom passed away, I was lost. Who would pray for me now? I felt like an orphan with not much family left, as I am single with no children. My mother's funeral was actually held at Saints Peter and Paul. Later, I went back there to regain a sense of connection to my family. I found a priest there to be my spiritual director.

---

2   Alessandro Baccari, Jr., Vincenza Scarpaci, Ph.D., and Rev. Father Gabriel Zavattaro, S.D.B., *Saints Peter & Paul Church, the Chronicles of "The Italian Cathedral" of the West, 1884-1984* (Published by Alessandro Baccari, Jr., for Saints Peter and Paul Church, c. 1985) 156–157.

He taught me that I'm never without a mother. My birth mother passed away, but Mother Mary is alive and well in my life. I can turn to Mary for prayer, emotional support, and a mother's unconditional love any time.

Perhaps it was Mary who led me back to the church that holds my family history and to the Madonna dei Miracoli. Now, when I pray and light a candle to her, I recognize that she is my spiritual mother, and I don't feel so alone.

It can be easy to fall into desolation when life gets challenging. But Mary teaches us to pray in those moments of despair. Not to give in or give up, but to pray, and even be willing to pray for a miracle. We can have faith because Jesus is a healer, and our God does mighty things.

At the Wedding at Cana, Mary told Jesus that the wedding party was out of wine. Because of her prompting, Jesus turned water into wine. This was his first miracle (see John 2:1–12), and it shows that no petition is too small to be worth his time, or his mother's notice. Of course, Jesus did many more miracles, as we read in Scripture. But he also does miracles in our lives, which we can always discover if we just search hard enough.

Do we acknowledge every miracle? No, not always. God's intervention in our lives can be very subtle, so much so that we do not even realize it. We can become nonchalant about the goodness of God, allowing his blessings and healings to go right over our heads. God is that amazing. But Mary our mother can help us recognize the miracles in our lives and give thanks for them. And she is always there, ready to hear our prayers and take them to her Son when we implore her help in any situation we may face. We can trust in the miraculous through Our Lady of Miracles.

That's what keeps me lighting candles. I go to Mary with the hope that my prayers will be answered, even if things do not turn out as I think they should. Mary helps me to trust that God knows best. I seek God's will, not mine, and I wait.

It is said that Christians have prayed using votive candles since ancient times. We pray to God or ask Mary and the saints for their intercession, and we light candles to keep our prayers burning long after we leave the church. People also light candles in thanksgiving for miracles that have already happened.

Msgr. Charles E. Pope writes that the candles we light hearken back to the Old Testament burnt offerings, in which "things of value . . . would be burned and thereby offered to God." We are offering something of value, symbolized by the candle, with our prayer or praise. Msgr. Pope adds, "The fire of the candle symbolizes ardent love. . . . The flickering light also seems to say, 'Remember me, Lord, remember my prayer and those for whom I pray.'"[3]

As I light my candles before the image of the Madonna dei Miracoli, I am grateful to have once again found refuge in this church where my family has prayed over the generations. Even though I won't carry on my family line with children, I do carry its faith—the faith of my great-grandmothers, grandmothers, and my mother. And I know that Mother Mary (and perhaps my own mother in heaven) prays for me and loves me, and I don't feel like an orphan spirit, alone in the world.

Mary is Our Lady of Miracles for the Church and also for me. Through her intercession, my life can be revived and regain its colorfulness, just as the statue of Nostra Signora dei Miracoli did, and I can bloom again, as did the wilted flowers on the altar in Cicagna.

Our Lady of Miracles, please pray for our intentions and be with us in our most desperate needs. We ask you to intercede for us with your son, Jesus Christ our Lord—he who performed so many miracles during his life on earth, and who continues to perform miracles for us from heaven. O Mary, we depend on your love as our Holy Mother to get us through the trials of our daily lives. Miracles are not out of reach for those who love you and Jesus. You care for us so lovingly, always. We place ourselves under your protection, and in ardent anticipation, Our Lady of Miracles, we beg you to pray for us! Amen.

---

3   Msgr. Charles E. Pope, "Why Are Votive Candles Used?" *Simply Catholic*, June 27, 2024, https://www.simplycatholic.com/why-are-votive-candles-used/.

Christine Arata strives to plant her fervent faith in her writing. Her goal is to inspire others to persevere through life's challenges and to have a thirst for the truth. She gets rejuvenated by nature, especially spending time near the Pacific Ocean and in nearby parks. Her tranquil and fragrant garden is her place of respite and joy. She has found purpose in promoting Saint Hildegard of Bingen, and you can learn more about that work at *sthildegardswisdom.com.*

VI

HOUSE OF GOLD

How Mary Pieced My Home and Heart Back Together

Lana Bergeron

*In this you rejoice, even if now for a little while you have
had to suffer various trials, so that the genuineness of
your faith—being more precious than gold that, though
perishable, is tested by fire—may be found to result in praise
and glory and honor when Jesus Christ is revealed.*

—1 Peter 1:6–7

The basket of clothes resembled a bowl of rising dough, appearing larger each time I passed by the laundry room. It was a random Tuesday morning in October, and most of the world was off in their place of work or school, while I was in our house, attempting the not so glamorous tasks of a stay-at-home mom. Suddenly, I heard a knock at the mudroom door.

Surprised to see company this early on a work day, I opened the door. Right away I noticed his usual smile was missing. I offered him coffee, and we sat together at the kitchen table, but his hands trembled, and he remained rigid, on the very edge of the chair, unable to look me in the eye for long. Finally, he blurted out, "I'm not really sure how to tell you this . . ."

After listening to his shocking message, I closed the door behind my friend as he left to return back to his home. The click of the door felt like an explosive fire that would not only burn every beautiful memory that was created in this house, but my family too.

All it took was one random, unexpected knock, and the home and family I had poured my heart and soul into was now covered in a layer of soot. In reality the outward appearance of our home had not been touched, but inside my heart was engulfed in flames so intense that I struggled to breathe. My eyes had become clouded from the smoke within, and all I could see was destruction. The foundation that I had sacrificed everything to build had vanished and had taken my heart along with it.

In the middle of the Litany of Loreto, we invoke Mary under a title that taps into the universal desire for a sense of home: House of Gold. Mary, who housed Jesus within her womb, can be compared to the ancient Temple—the house King Solomon built for the Lord in the Old Testament.

We read in the first book of Kings, "And Solomon overlaid the inside of the house with pure gold, and he drew chains of gold across, in front of the inner sanctuary, and overlaid it with gold" (I Kings 6:21).

Gold is often considered the most precious of metals because it does not corrode. It remains true in colour and can even be molded into something new and beautiful when held over a flame. Nothing could be as fitting as gold for the construction of the dwelling place of the Lord. Mary is truly the House of Gold because, free from the impurities of sin and filled with unparalleled beauty, she housed the unborn child Jesus.

Mary as House of Gold is foreshadowed in the Old Testament by the Ark of the Covenant. The ark was a wooden chest plated in gold that housed the most sacred symbols of the covenant God made with the chosen people. Inside were the Ten Commandments, the manna, and the priestly rod of Aaron. Dr. Scott Hahn writes,

Whatever made the ark holy made Mary even holier. If the first ark contained the Word of God in stone, Mary's body contained the Word of God enfleshed. If the first ark contained miraculous bread from heaven, Mary's body contained the very Bread of Life that conquers death forever. If the first ark contained the rod of the long-ago ancestral priest, Mary's body contained the divine person of the eternal priest, Jesus Christ.[1]

For centuries, the title "House of Gold" whispered of Mary, who would be the ultimate tabernacle, the new Ark of the Covenant, housing the sacred Presence that the Jewish people guarded so fiercely. The inner vessel that Mary housed was so pure that no darkness could penetrate its gilded surface.

The darkness that had landed on my doorstep that autumn morning, however, began to creep into every crevice of our home, into every interior room of my mind, and even into my body. Trying to hide the shame and betrayal from everyone I knew, I finally broke down over a phone call from my cousin during the holidays. I somehow managed to blurt out the word *affair* for the first time. At first it was met with a long, dead silence. We spoke only a few words after that, but the one thing she could think to offer was a gift I've cherished every day since.

She had started saying the Rosary with a group she had stumbled upon on Instagram called Many Hail Marys at a Time. She knew there was nothing she could do to help me save our marriage, but she sent me the group's Instagram handle, thus pointing me to the only woman she knew who could help: our Mother Mary. This beautiful online community led by two sisters has been praying the Rosary daily for over seven years. Hundreds join them live every morning, and many have joined them to share the work Mary has done in their own lives.

---

1   Scott Hahn, *Hail, Holy Queen: The Mother of God in the Word of God* (New York: Doubleday, 2001), 60.

I entrusted my plea for redemption and restoration to Mary through the daily Rosary. I also prayed in front of Jesus' Eucharistic presence in the tabernacle at church, and with the help of both of these practices, slowly the process of healing began. It took a great deal of time, along with a retreat, therapy, life coaching, and other means of healing, but in the end our marriage and home were rebuilt.

Dealing with betrayal was undoubtedly the biggest struggle I have ever faced. The topic is not often talked about, and as a result often silently destroys its victims. Doing the hard work to repair our marriage and to welcome forgiveness under the watchful eye of the Lord through his mother, I began to see that up until everything fell apart, my life had been ordered incorrectly. It is not that I didn't love God or my husband, but I poured myself into my role as a stay-at-home mom, and I had made that my priority. Struggling to find worth in a world that values career and success left me feeling unworthy.

As I began to reorder the importance of the tabernacle of my heart, things drastically changed. The first priority needed to be my relationship with God. Only through partnering with him did the golden glimmers of healing start to surface. Next needed to be the relationship with my husband, focusing on connection and communication. Then came the third level which I had previously listed on top of everything and everyone else: our family. After all, my life started with God, then came my vocation of marriage, followed by the blessing of our family. As soon as things were ordered correctly, those feelings of unworthiness began to dwindle.

The Japanese have created a beautiful artform known as *Kintsugi,* which translates to "golden repair." Instead of getting rid of broken pottery or repairing it in a way that hides any cracks, Kintsugi repairs the pottery by highlighting cracks with a gold lacquer, making the pottery even more beautiful and often more valuable than before. As difficult as it is to share an easily judged story, I know that my marriage now is like the repaired pottery, highlighting our healing and offering hope.

My hope is that others who find themselves silently struggling can find the courage to trust the Lord and Mary to show them how beauty truly can come from ashes. Granted, every marriage is unique, and the outcome from betrayal will be different for each couple who goes through it. I am grateful that I had a partner who wanted to work things out, just as I did. But what is universal for us all is God's invitation to dwell with him. Welcoming God into the deepest rooms of our hearts rebuilds that which is broken and renovates our lives. Just as the center of Mary's House of Gold was Jesus, when we place him in the sanctuary of our own hearts, our lives begin to radiate love that then pours out into the world as a source of light for others.

God knocked on my door in the most unimaginable and at that time excruciatingly painful way that October morning, but welcoming him in has given me a marriage I could only have dreamed of. Thank you, Mother Mary, for restoring our home with all of your golden graces.

Having experienced the healing and restorative power of grace in her own life, **Lana Bergeron** is blessed to mentor women and help them rediscover and reclaim the sacred space within where God dwells, designing lives of faith and flourishing. She works as a life coach from her home in Ontario and can be contacted at *lanabergeron.com*.

VII

Our Lady of Compassion

How Mary Abides with Us in Our Suffering

Brittany Brosdahl

And a sword will pierce your own soul too.

—Luke 2:35

Kneeling in adoration for the first time years ago, I consecrated myself to Jesus through Mary. My heart burned as she helped me perceive Jesus in the Blessed Sacrament. And as I knelt there, Jesus entrusted me to her.

In his deepest suffering, Christ pointed us to Mary: "When Jesus saw his mother and the disciple whom he loved standing beside her, he said to his mother, 'Woman, here is your son.' Then he said to the disciple, 'Here is your mother.' And from that hour the disciple took her into his own home" (John 19:26–27). St. John Paul II describes this entrustment as an invitation to let Mary into the home of our heart: "The Apostle John, 'welcomes' the Mother of Christ 'into his own home' and brings her into everything that makes up his inner life, that is to say into his human and Christian 'I': he 'took her to his own home.'"[1]

---

1   John Paul II, *Redemptoris Mater* (On the Blessed Virgin Mary in the life of the Pilgrim Church), n. 45, https://www.vatican.va/content/john-paul-ii/en/encyclicals/documents/hf_jp-ii_enc_25031987_redemptoris-mater.html

When I first consecrated myself to Mary, I didn't know her very well. But I wanted to. Jesus gave her to me, so she must be important. In faith, I opened the door of my heart to her.

Yet as I've grown in relationship with Mary over the years, I've encountered barriers in my heart. Mary is perfect, free from sin. At times I wondered, "Can she truly understand me? Can I go to her with *everything*? Does she really 'get it'?" Mary draws near to us, but she can seem lofty and distant, can't she? It's easy to keep her at arm's length.

In spite of my doubts, Mary remained with me, nourishing my fiat, as she does for each of her children. In *Redemptoris Mater,* John Paul II says, "The Virgin Mother is constantly present on this journey of faith of the People of God towards the light."[2] Making a pilgrimage to the Shrine of Our Lady of Champion was a turning point in our relationship. I became aware of Mary's abiding presence on my journey toward the light of Christ. In Mary, I found a mother who sees me and knows me completely, and still she stays with me. She remains at my side. And more than this, she enters into my story. She suffers all things with me.

Mary's presence is filled with compassion. *Compassion* is taken from the Latin word *cum,* meaning "with" or "together," and from the Latin verb *patior,* meaning "to suffer." *Compassion* can be defined as "to suffer with."

The title "Our Lady of Compassion" is the first to have been associated with Mary's sorrows. The Church invites us to contemplate how she suffered with Christ. Her compassionate heart is deeply affiliated with the Cross, for it is in his crucifixion that Jesus gives us Our Lady of Compassion.

Mary is present in our interior journey through the Cross: "The pilgrimage of faith indicates the interior history, that is, the story of souls."[3] On pilgrimage to Wisconsin, I grew in awareness of how Mary

---

2 Ibid., n. 35.
3 John Paul II, "Redemptoris Mater: On the Blessed Virgin Mary in the life of the Pilgrim Church," n. 6

draws near to me in my personal story. As I asked her intercession, I saw how she cares about my circumstances. My history.

Little by little, step by step, I realized I didn't have to hide my heart from her. I could bring her *everything*. All my honest needs, wounds, sorrows, hopes, fears, desires, joys. She receives them. She enters my story, including my stories of suffering.

I saw how through her intercession, everything can be transformed in Christ. She goes with her children *through* the Cross. She brings us the hope of uniting all pain to Christ's, transforming our hearts in him. Being on pilgrimage awakened me to Mary's presence in this sacred process. It opened me up to an awareness of my deeper need for interior healing.

At a time when Jesus was calling me into the journey of healing the deepest wounds in my heart, I made a visit to the Art Institute of Chicago. He drew me closer to Our Lady of Compassion through the art I beheld there. I saw my need for her more clearly and let her deeper into the home of my heart. I saw how Mary brings her healing presence into the darkness. Transfigured by her union with him, she herself is luminous and full of compassion. Through her, I felt Christ's presence.

I recall Rembrandt's drawing *Christ Crucified Between the Two Thieves: The Three Crosses*.[4] The scene is covered in darkness. Still, the tenderness and compassion of Christ's infinite love permeates this piece. A light breaks through from above, washing over Christ crucified.

Gazing at him, I had the impression of Christ descending into the depths of all betrayal, abandonment, despair, anguish, sorrow, harm, trauma. Psychiatrist Gabore Mate says, "Children don't get traumatized because they are hurt. Children are traumatized because they are alone with the hurt."[5] Trauma is understood as being alone in pain. But in

---

4 Rembrandt von Rijn, *Christ Crucified between the Two Thieves: "The Three Crosses,"* 1653, Art Institute Chicago, https://www.artic.edu/artworks/80077/christ-crucified-between-the-two-thieves-the-three-crosses.

5 Maurizio Benazzo and Zaya Benazzo, directors, *The Wisdom of Trauma* (Sausalito, CA: Science and Nonduality, 2021).

Rembrandt's work, I saw that Christ has not left us alone in our trauma. He entered our wounds. The light of Christ has broken into the darkness. He came to be with us.

In the same way, Mary does not leave her children alone. Our Lady of Compassion descended into the darkness with her son. She did not leave him alone. At the foot of the Cross, Mother Mary stood with Christ at the heart and center of the great undoing of all trauma. It's as though, together, Jesus and Mary broke through the wounds of betrayal and abandonment. They entered our suffering, together. Mary is with Jesus in his great mission of healing humanity and enfolding us into the loving Heart of the Father. Through her compassionate presence, she brings the light of Christ into suffering. She abides with each one of us.

In Rembrandt's drawing, a crowd surrounds the Cross. In the darkness, there is chaos. The crowd is filled with distraction. The people's hearts are far away from Christ. They don't recognize him. They don't believe he is who he says he is. This is God, crucified. Perfect communion in himself, betrayed. The crowd around him doesn't receive him. They don't believe he is Love. But at the crucifixion there was someone who saw him. Who knew him. Who believed in him.

Moving on from Rembrandt's work, I was captivated by Filippo Parodi's sculpture of the *Pietà*.[6] Mary stands, leaning over her Son's dead body, in a gesture of receiving him into her arms. She was the first and last to hold him. Compelled by faith, she had followed him into the deepest suffering. She entered in at the foot of the Cross as a believing witness. She pressed into his story of betrayal. I was captivated and drawn deeply into this piece. I felt deep in my bones how *this woman knows me*.

In the sculpture, Mary gazes down at Christ. While others don't see and believe, she knows who this is. This is her innocent Son—a divine victim.

---

6   Filippo Parodi, *Pietá*, c. 1686, Art Institute Chicago, https://www.artic.edu/artworks/160235/pieta.

Trauma can be defined as "unwitnessed pain."[7] Mary heals with her witness. In her steadfast abiding, she beheld Jesus in his suffering. She didn't turn away. She knew the extent of the harm. In love, she witnessed to the truth, and she gave Jesus her compassionate presence. In her book *Handmaid of the Lord*, Adrienne von Speyr beautifully describes the "mystery of presence." She says it "has its roots in Mary's presence at the foot of the Cross and makes assistance in suffering and death a tactful act of love."[8]

The mystery of the loving presence of another is revealed through Our Lady of Compassion. With her, suffering becomes meaningful. For, "Suffering is fruitful and compassion is a grace. For Mother and Son it is a gift to be allowed to suffer together."[9] Presence heals. It says, "I see you, and I'm not leaving. I'm in it with you. I receive you. You're loved in your wounds." Mary doesn't bypass the pain of the Cross. She doesn't make excuses for the harm. She doesn't avoid, diminish, fix, explain or provide solutions. Mary shows us the dignity, strength and hope found in suffering. She makes space for truth to emerge. She reveals our hearts to us, awakening our longing for Christ. *She suffers with.*

Gazing upon Our Lady of Compassion as she gazed at her son, I intuited how she never abandons me. I knew to my core that she will always be a witness to the truth of my story, making room for me to speak my truth. She will stand with me and for me. I understood how she cares for me, her child. Looking at her, I saw how my suffering is her own.

Christ drew Mary's compassionate heart deeply into his suffering. At the foot of the Cross, the prophecy of Simeon was fulfilled: "And a sword will pierce your own soul too" (Luke 2:35).

His heart was pierced with love and mercy. Her heart was pierced with his.

---

7 Dr. Alison Cook, "What Are the Effects of Trauma?," accessed October 8, 2025, https://www.dralisoncook.com/blog/what-are-the-effects-of-trauma.

8 Adrienne von Speyr, *Handmaid of the Lord* (San Francisco: Ignatius Press, 2017), 135.

9 Ibid.

John Paull II describes her sharing in his deepest anguish: "the Mother endured 'with her only-begotten Son the intensity of his suffering, associated herself with his sacrifice in her mother's heart' . . . the Council reminds us of 'Mary's compassion'; in her heart reverberates all that Jesus suffers in body and soul."[10] In suffering, they were united. Their hearts were one.

The Immaculate Heart of Mary, pierced by the sword, is filled with tenderness and empathy for her children. Her heart is pierced with our hearts. She takes our pain into her heart and lives it with us, thus transforming the hurting parts of our hearts through her compassionate heart.

Our Lady of Compassion loves unconditionally. In her heart, she stands with her children—she stands with you. She's on your side. When she looks at you, she sees Christ in you. She sees the innocence in your suffering. She sees your deepest, truest identity in Christ: *child of the Father.* Her gaze sees your fullest potential. She *believes* in you.

Mother Mary's Immaculate Heart makes room for the human heart to unfold—to be seen, known, understood, healed, *transformed.*

When I arrived at the Shrine of Our Lady of Champion, I was surprised to find that new prayer intentions had surfaced in my heart. My faith had expanded. I asked for graces I had never hoped to ask for. Mary had purified and transformed my desires. I realized my deepest desire for the light of Christ to break into my story. Mary helps us see that our journey isn't aimless. We are destined for eternal Beatitude.

With Mother Mary, Our Lady of Compassion, I cannot walk alone.

Litany to Our Lady of Compassion

Our Lady of Compassion,
you suffered with your son at the foot of the Cross.
You stood steadfast with him in faith, hope, and love.
You didn't leave him alone.

---

10 John Paul II, "Mary United Herself to Jesus' Offering," General Audience, April 2, 1997, n. 2.

Together, your hearts were pierced.
In your Immaculate Heart, pierced by the sword,
you suffered with me, your little child.

Mother Mary, full of compassion,
I welcome you into the home of my heart.
Stand with me at the foot of my cross.
Abide with me in my pain.
Witness to the hurting parts of my heart.
Suffer with me. Take my pain into your heart.

When I am betrayed,
abide with me.

When I am abandoned,
abide with me.

When my heart is scourged,
abide with me.

When I am grief-stricken,
abide with me.

When I am sorrowful unto death,
abide with me.

When I grow weary and discouraged,
abide with me.

When all feels lost, stolen, taken, and my garments are divided among them,
abide with me.

When my body feels broken,
abide with me.

When I am mocked, judged, scorned, ridiculed, and criticized,
abide with me.

When I am forsaken,
abide with me.

When I am overwhelmed,
abide with me. Bring me peace.

When I am afraid,
abide with me. Bring me courage.

When the weight seems too heavy,
abide with me. Give me strength.

Mother most compassionate,
stand steadfast beside me. Stand with me in truth.

When I am manipulated,
stand with me in truth.

When I am confused,
bring me clarity. Stand with me in truth.

When I am doubted,
believe me. Stand with me in truth.

When I feel unseen,
see me.

When I feel unknown,
show me how I am known to my core.

When I am not heard,
hear me. Listen to the cry of my heart.

When I am misunderstood,
understand me.

When I am silenced,
help me speak my truth.

When I am rejected,
receive me.

When I am cast out,
accept me.

When I am discouraged,
encourage me.

When I am controlled,
honor my freedom and dignity.

When my conscience is invaded,
Reverence the sacred ground of my heart. Cultivate space in my soul.

When I am undefended,
defend, guard and protect me.

When I am not believed in,
believe in me.

When I am belittled,
raise me up to your tender gaze and love me in my littleness.

When I feel like I'm not enough,
hold me close to your heart. Show me I am worthy.

When I feel broken,
affirm the truth of my goodness.

When I feel used,
love me unconditionally.

Our Lady of Compassion,
validate my feelings. Feel them with me. Process my emotions with me.

When my justified anger is suppressed,
be angry with me.

When my sorrow is too great,
weep with me. Soothe my sorrow.

When I am abused,
enfold me into your Immaculate Heart.

Mother Mary, Our Lady of Compassion,
be a healing presence for me now.
Bring the light of Christ into the darkness.
Help me receive the tears that flow for me from your heart,
pierced and wounded by the sword of sorrows.
Help me to know the compassion of the pierced Heart of Christ.
Show me how the mercy that flows from his heart is love.
Unite every ounce of my suffering to Christ's Cross,
transforming my heart into his.
Awaken within me new joy, creativity, and playfulness.
Make me fruitful.

Mother of Compassion, abide with me into the light of the Resurrection.
Lead me into the loving Heart of the Father.

Brittany Brosdahl is passionate about the interior life and how our hearts are nourished and healed. She has a master's degree in Catholic Studies from the University of St. Thomas. While working on her thesis about Mary's compassion, she was deeply moved by how profoundly present Mother Mary is in our journeys toward healing in Christ. Find the litany and follow her at *Immaculatehearthealing.substack.com.*

VIII

Salve Regina

Walking with Mary and Seeking Mercy

Beth Casteel

Salve Regína, mater misericordiæ;
vita, dulcedo, et spes nostra, salve!
Ad te clamamus, exsules filii Evæ.
Ad te suspiramus, gementes et flentes
in hac lacrimarum valle.
Eia ergo, Advocata nostra,
illos tuos misericordes oculos
ad nos converte.
Et Iesum, benedictum fructum ventris tui,
nobis post hoc exsílium ostende.
O clemens, O pia, O dulcis Virgo María!

Not long after I celebrated my forty-seventh birthday, my body rebelled. Up until the spring of 2012, I had few health concerns. I actively cared for our four children, kept a busy volunteer schedule, and was training for a half marathon when several weirdly debilitating ailments began. I had unrelenting heart palpitations and could feel the missed fourth beat like a butterfly in my throat; extreme nausea caused me to lose twenty pounds; and worst of all, a nerve-like pain radiated from my neck down my left shoulder and into my back. I struggled to drive the car. Twice I doubled over in pain and had to be taken to the emergency room.

My doctor shot me with steroids and sent me for GI tests, and then to get my gall bladder out, a week before our oldest daughter graduated from high school. The neurologist could not find the source of the shoulder pain but ordered physical therapy. My cardiologist hospitalized me for three days after my heart monitor transmitted unusual activity, and an ambulance sped me, lights flashing, the EMT fumbling to get my IV started, from our rural community to the northside of Pittsburgh in a frenetic seventy-five-minute ride. The one doctor who provided solid answers for why this was happening was my cardiologist—the only female doctor in the bunch—who suggested that it all was probably related to the onset of menopause.

Many sleepless, pain-filled nights, I gripped the olive wood rosary that my parents brought back from Medjugorje so hard that the little carvings in each bead left indentations on my fingers. Reruns of Mother Angelica's EWTN television show shed light into the dark family room, and I grew attached to the Hail, Holy Queen—the prayer said at the conclusion of the Rosary:

Hail, Holy Queen, Mother of Mercy,
our life, our sweetness and our hope.
To thee do we cry,
poor banished children of Eve.
To thee do we send up our sighs,
mourning and weeping in this valley of tears.
Turn then, most gracious advocate,
thine eyes of mercy toward us,
and after this our exile
show unto us the blessed fruit of thy womb, Jesus.
O clement, O loving,
O sweet Virgin Mary.

While the Hail Marys lulled me into the Blessed Mother's arms, the words of the Hail, Holy Queen allowed me to feel recognized in this period of pain that stalled my life. If the "Hail Mary" reflected the perfection of our Mother, the Hail, Holy Queen invited me, fallen and suffering, into her sanctuary.

The Hail, Holy Queen is the English translation of the Latin *Salve Regina,* one of four Marian antiphons traditionally sung after Compline (Night Prayer in the Liturgy of the Hours). Each of the four antiphons is assigned to a different season in the Church's liturgical calendar. *Alma Redemptoris Mater* is sung from the first Sunday in Advent to February 2, the Feast of the Purification or Candlemas; *Ave Regina Caelorum,* from Candlemas to the Easter Vigil; *Regina Caeli,* from the Easter Vigil to Pentecost; and *Salve Regina* from the day after Pentecost Sunday until the first Sunday of Advent.[1]

"The Salve Regina, after the Hail Mary, is undoubtedly the best-known and most-loved Marian prayer within the Catholic tradition," writes Fr. Robert Nixon, OSB. "It is recited at the conclusion of each mystery of the rosary; and, for those in monastic and consecrated life, it is traditionally sung as a final antiphon at night after compline, throughout most seasons of the year."[2]

Debate continues regarding composition of the *Salve Regina,* with some musicologists attributing the antiphon to an anonymous author. Most scholars credit Blessed Hermannus Contractus (1013–1034), or Herman of Reichenau, with authorship.[3] Blessed Herman was a renowned scholar of his time and wrote on many complex subjects, including musical

---

1 Lucy E. Carroll, "Singing the Four Seasonal Marian Hymns," *Adoremus,* September 15, 2007.

2 Fr. Robert Nixon, OSB, "The Author of the Salve Regina: The Stories of Two Great Lovers of Mary," Tan Direction, 2023, https://tandirection.com/pursuit-of-perfection/the-author-of-the-salve-regina-the-stories-of-two-great-lovers-of-mary/.

3 "Salve, Regina (Hail, Mary)," https://hymnary.org/text/hail_mary_mother_and_queen_of_tender.

theory. Some sources say Herman was born with physical difficulties, while others claim he had disabilities as a result of a childhood illness.

Some speculate that the last lines of the *Salve Regina* ("*O clemens, O pia, O dulcis Virgo Maria!*", translated as "O clement, O loving, O sweet Virgin Mary!") were written by St. Bernard of Clairvaux (1090–1153). One source relates: "On entering the Dom, the Salve Regina was intoned with the greatest enthusiasm. St. Bernard was deeply moved, and as the last words resounded: 'After this our exile show unto us the blessed fruit of thy womb, Jesus,' the saint exclaimed: 'O clemens, O pia, O dulcis Virgo Maria'—'O clement, O loving, O sweet Virgin Mary.'"[4]

St. Alphonsus Liguori (1696–1787) relied heavily upon the writings of St. Bernard and other saints when he wrote *The Glories of Mary* in defense of Our Lady's elevated position in the Catholic Church, during a time when many scholars were critical of Marian devotion and had special disdain for the *Salve Regina*.[5] The first section of *The Glories of Mary* is devoted to the *Salve Regina*:

> I say on the mercy of Mary: for St. Bernard says, we may praise her humility, and marvel at her virginity; but being poor sinners, we are more pleased and attracted by hearing of her mercy; for to this we more affectionately cling, this we more often remember and invoke.[6]

He goes on to address why the Church gives Mary the title Queen of Mercy:

> Because we believe that she throws open the abyss of God's mercies to anyone she pleases, when she pleases, and as she pleases. Hence, there

---

4 "The Origin of the 'Salve Regina,'" *Sacred Heart Review* 9, no. 4 (December 17,1892), https://newspapers.bc.edu/?a=d&d=BOSTONSH18921217-01.2.56&e=-------en-20--1--txt-txIN------.

5 "An Explanation of the Salve Regina by St. Alphonsus Liguori, *The Glories of Mary* Excerpts, https://www.prayinglatin.com/an-explanation-of-the-salve-regina-by-st-alphonsus-liguori/.

6 St. Alphonso Maria de Liguori, *The Glories of Mary* (P.J. Kenedy, New York, 1888), 21, https://archive.org/details/thegloriesofmary00liguuoft/page/20/mode/2up.

are no sinners who will be lost—no matter how great their crimes—when this most holy Lady intercedes for them.[7]

Going to Mary in prayer does not guarantee Catholics a seat at the heavenly banquet, but I believe that she leads me to the fount of mercy that is inexhaustible, despite my constant retreat into a valley populated by failure, sin, complaint, and ingratitude. My love for Our Lady stems from a need to be shown the blessed fruit of her womb, Jesus, to be given understanding for his Incarnation, his life as a carpenter's son, his years of preaching and endowing his best friends with his mission, and his brutal death on the Cross. She accompanies me as I struggle to accept the mercy wrought for me on the Cross.

So many of us are trapped in dysfunctional relationships, poverty, communities we dislike, difficult jobs, deteriorating bodies, and debilitated minds. We sit in prisons built of unworthiness, unable to grasp that our cellblocks have been freed by the repetitive receipt of holy mercy. The "Salve Regina" gave me, a poor banished child in her late forties who had scars from infertility and struggles with anxiety and depression, hope in spaces that felt barren. It allowed me space to grieve, with mourning and weeping, the suffering one of our children was enduring at that time.

The Latin *Salve* is translated most literally as "Hail," but the dictionary definitions of the English word *salve*—"healing balm" and "to save from loss and destruction"—are what I seek when I am deep in prayer with Our Lady.[8] Though this year of weird ailments was not the heaviest cross I have carried, it taught me what to do with suffering. Rote prayer can be a soothing remedy in times of desolation. Praying the Rosary through the intense periods of pain that punctured my life showed me that I could rely on God in difficult times.

---

7   *The Glories of Mary* excerpts, https://www.prayinglatin.com/an-explanation-of-the-salve-regina-by-st-alphonsus-liguori/.

8   "Salve," https://www.dictionary.com/browse/salve.

It also reminded me to embrace joy. As an organist, I have often been shocked by the gusto with which our church members sing the Hail, Holy Queen. Catholics are not known for roof-raising hymn sings, but give them a Marian feast day and accompanying hymn, and you will be swept up in the praise and exultation of "Hail, Holy Queen enthroned above, O Maria. Hail, Queen of Mercy and of Love, O Maria. Triumph all ye cherubim! Sing with us ye seraphim! Heaven and hearth resound the hymn. Salve, Salve, Salve Regina."

Hail, Holy Queen is the spoken prayer that pacifies, protects, and upholds me in this last third of life. It is words murmured prior to Mass and before I go to sleep, an a cappella chant sung by our choir director after communion, the stanzas I have played, full organ, as congregations were sent off to proclaim the Gospel.

My physical ailments of 2012 did come to an end. By 2013, I regained full health, ran the half marathon, and was able to quit taking the heart medication for the palpitations. But those intense periods of physical suffering taught me how to persevere under the weight of the cross: by leaning on Mary's constant intercession, trusting that, even as I linger in this valley of tears, I can trust in the promise of mercy, and the blessed fruit she will surely show unto me after this, my exile.

Beth Casteel searches for truth in the messiness of life. She worked as a journalist and earned an MFA in creative nonfiction from Carlow University, but her greatest calling has been to motherhood. Beth has been an organist for forty years. She serves in various church ministries and as a community volunteer. You can interact with her at *bethcasteel.com*.

IX

Our Lady of Beauraing

How Mary Remains Our Constant Companion in Prayer

Kate Eschbach

*All these were constantly devoting themselves to
prayer, together with certain women, including Mary
the mother of Jesus, as well as his brothers.*

—Acts 1:14

As the train pulled out of the station in Brussels, I looked over to see my son, Riley, watching intently out the window. The train rattled through the tunnels, past concrete and graffiti, then emerged next to a quiet canal. We meandered with the water as peaceful green hills watched us roll by. The train swayed with a soothing rhythm, and I took a deep breath, trusting God's hands to guide this pilgrimage.

My husband and I had decided to learn how to navigate the Belgian train system by taking this day trip in the middle of our pilgrimage trip to Geel to pray for healing for my son, Riley. Brussels served as our temporary home base as we acclimated to the new time zone and found our way around.

Months before, I had called my sister-in-law, Laura, to ask her for travel advice. She had lived internationally in college and is now a seasoned traveler. A few days after our phone call, she sent me a text. Did I know there were two approved Marian apparition sites in Belgium? Beauraing and Banneux. I had never heard of them!

We decided Beauraing would be the perfect day trip.

Many years ago, my husband and I dreamt of teaching English abroad. Brian spoke French beautifully, and we wanted to travel together after we were married. We no longer dreamed of living across the ocean, but the thought of putting his French to good use sounded like fun. Beauraing is located only four miles from the French border, and the locals speak French and English. Knowing Brian could communicate with everyone, traveling to Beauraing felt like a safe decision to practice our train navigation skills. It wasn't too far from Brussels, and it would be great practice for when we took the train to Geel, the home of St. Dymphna—our final pilgrimage destination.

I learned of St. Dymphna in 2015 when I found a holy card in my bedroom. I had never heard of her, and I do not know how the holy card (written in Spanish) ended up in my room. After that, I continued to find St. Dymphna everywhere. She showed up in art in New Mexico on a trip with my college roommate, in book recommendations, and even in a thrift store—but those are stories for another day. In my reading, I learned that she had fled from Ireland to Geel, Belgium. Geel has a cathedral and welcomes pilgrims from all over the world every year to pray for healing, specifically for mental health.

The train had rocked my son to sleep. He was looking less like a little boy and more like a young man. I took this quiet moment to breathe deeply and ask the Holy Spirit to be with us. I begged God to help us and heal the early development trauma that Riley faced. Like a child tugging on a sleeve, reminding her parents of the ice cream she wants, my heart cried out to God, reminding him that I wanted healing for Riley.

Many years ago, my husband and I had set a goal to "research adoption." Words scribbled on a page of goals became a reality for our family four months after writing them. We began fostering Riley when he was two years old. At three and a half, Riley officially became an Eschbach. The judge proclaimed, "It's a boy!" and everyone in the courtroom laughed and hugged.

We knew the Lord had guided our hearts to this little one. However, we were blissfully naïve about the developmental trauma and attachment disorders that could happen with adoption. We believed that if we prayed and loved enough, our story would have a beautiful ending, and everyone would live happily ever after.

After trying every type of therapy we could find, doctors eventually diagnosed Riley with Reactive Attachment Disorder. This means that attaching to a new caregiver would be incredibly difficult, maybe impossible. It also meant that everything we had been doing as a family to build trust and a relationship with him was actually causing more damage. The closer I tried to get to him, through nurturing and quality time, the less in control he felt.

It was maddening. Outside the home, our family appeared to be completely normal. But when the front door shut, and no one else could see, our home looked nothing like the hopes and dreams I had held for my family. Rage and the need for control ruled his responses to the sound of my voice. In Eucharistic adoration one day, I found myself heartbroken, crying out to God for help. I had taken Riley to the chapel after a particularly terrible episode that left me shaken and scared. "God, he is a child. This isn't fair. Help me!" I screamed.

Now, sitting on the train to Beauraing, I took a deep breath and shook the memory out of my head.

The train slowed down, and we pulled up to the train station in Beauraing. It was quiet. Little yellow flowers dotted the fields, and there was a warm glow over everything. Was this the warmth the Flemish painters so masterfully captured on canvas? Red poppies lined the wooden train station. After the train departed, the only sound was the crunch of the gravel beneath our feet.

We followed the sidewalk to a cafe and took a seat inside. Brian and the owner exchanged introductions, and he ordered the most delicious sandwich—a croque monsieur. The cafe patrons were curious and kind and pointed us on our way.

The town was installing a roundabout, so we carefully navigated through the construction. There were workers shouting and wooden boards covering unsafe parts of the sidewalk as we marched single file toward a distant Hawthorn tree. It all seemed familiar and foreign, to wander through the mundane to reach an encounter with the Divine.

Before this trip, the only Marian apparition site I really knew of was Lourdes. Thinking Beauraing would be similar, I expected lines of people and nervous excitement. Instead, we found a visitor's center with one employee. She greeted us joyfully and showed us the drawings the children had made of their encounter with Our Lady. She showed us the school and the courtyard and invited us to stay as long as we wanted. She also showed us the stage that had been built when Pope St. John Paul II visited.

While preparing for our trip, I had been so focused on Geel that I had not taken time to learn about Beauraing. The peace captivated my heart and overwhelmed me. I wandered the grounds quietly and read the material we had received at the visitor's center.

From November 29, 1932, to January 3, 1933, five children ranging in age from nine to fifteen experienced a series of thirty-three Marian apparitions. The Blessed Virgin appeared youthful and radiant, dressed in white and surrounded by a luminous blue light. The apparitions often took place near a convent schoolyard, and as news of the children's visions spread, crowds of pilgrims gathered—sometimes up to 30,000 people—to witness the events and join in prayer.[1]

I gasped. Thirty thousand people? It wasn't that long ago. How had I not heard about this?

---

1   Joseph Pronechen, "Who Is Our Lady of Beauraing—and What Is Her Connection to Alaska?" *National Catholic Register*, November 10, 2024, https://www.ncregister.com/features/our-lady-of-beauraing-primer.

The five children would drop to their knees in ecstasy. Doctors conducted tests to ascertain whether the children were simply acting, including pinching their calves hard, pushing a knife into one of the visionary's skin, and burning another's hands with a match. The children remained completely unaffected.

During one encounter, Mary affirmed her title as the "Immaculate Virgin" and asked the children simply "that you always be good." In later apparitions, she requested that a chapel be built in her honor, and she revealed her heart shining with golden light—a symbol that gave rise to the title "Our Lady of the Golden Heart."

On the final day, Mary entrusted the children with messages of conversion, prayer, and self-sacrifice. She vowed to convert sinners and encouraged constant prayer, and her golden heart radiated with remarkable brilliance.

To one child, Fernande, Mary asked, "Do you love my son? Do you love me? Then sacrifice yourself for me."[2]

The apparitions inspired a surge of devotion in Belgium, with ecclesial investigations eventually leading to the authorization of public veneration and recognition of miracles attributed to her intercession. Today, the shrine at Beauraing remains a place of pilgrimage and prayer, radiating Mary's call to goodness and deeper love for her Son.

I wandered to the chapel and found a group of nuns adorning the altar with beautiful flowers. I sat down in a chair and smiled. They were using daisies—big pink gerbera daisies, just like the ones on my wedding cake. In this quiet moment, I knew God was reminding me that he sees me.

In 1985, when Pope St. John Paul II celebrated Mass in Beauraing, he said, "The whole Church, after the Ascension of the Lord, returns to the Upper Room to await in prayer the descent of the Holy Spirit on the day of Pentecost: it is at this chosen moment that we come to Beauraing. We

---

2   "Our Lady of the Golden Heart," https://www.piercedhearts.org/hearts_jesus_mary/apparitions/our_lady_beauraing.html.

come here to be assiduous in praying with one heart, like the Apostles, with Mary, the Mother of the Lord (Acts 1:14)."[3] This is what Mary had to teach me during that brief trip to Beauraing: to keep going in prayer, even when it felt like our prayers had no effect.

Our Belgian pilgrimage continued. We visited the Basilica of the Holy Blood in Bruges, and we ended the pilgrimage in Geel, the home of St. Dymphna. The priest in Geel welcomed us like family. Our experience changed all three of us in beautiful, meaningful ways. But was Riley miraculously healed? No.

The more I've thought about our visit to Belgium, I've come to realize that of course St. Dymphna introduced us to Our Lady of Beauraing, Our Lady of the Golden Heart. All this time, I've thought the purpose of our pilgrimage was to visit Geel and the Church of St. Dymphna. But I think there is more. Just as the saints lead us to Christ, they also remind us of the tenderness and sweetness of his mother. She never left Christ's side in his suffering, and she will not leave us, either. She is a constant companion, reminding us to call upon the Lord, just like she did with the apostles in the upper room, just like she did with the children of Beauraing when she asked them to "pray, pray, pray."

Sometimes, heaven brushes close to earth in ways we almost miss, like the winter evenings in Beauraing almost a hundred years ago, when five children listened intently to Our Lady under bare Hawthorn branches.

Let us walk forward with hope, knowing that Mary is near to us, telling us: you are seen, you are loved, and remember to pray.

---

3 St. John Paul II, homily at Beauraing, May 18, 1985, https://www.vatican.va/content/john-paul-ii/fr/homilies/1985/documents/hf_jp-ii_hom_19850518_beauraing.html.

Prayer to Our Lady of Beauraing

Our Lady of Beauraing, Immaculate Virgin, carry to
Jesus, your Son, all the intentions which we confide
to you this day. (*Here mention your intentions.*)

Mother with the Golden Heart, mirror of the tenderness
of the Father, look with love upon the men and women of
our time and fill them with the joy of your presence.

You who promised to convert sinners, help us
discover the infinite mercy of our God. Awaken
in us the grace of conversion so that all our life
becomes the reflection of this mercy.

Holy Mother of God, look down upon our miseries, console
us in our sorrows, give strength to all those who are suffering.

Queen of Heaven, crowned with light, help us grow in faith,
hope and love, and we shall be able to give thanks without end.

You brought Jesus into the world; may we, by prayer, by
sharing his word and by the testimony of our life filled
with love and joy make him be born in all hearts.

May every instant of our life be a Yes to the question, which
you are asking us today: Do you love my son? Do you love me?
Then the reign of Jesus will come into the world. Amen.[4]

---

4   Prayer to Our Lady of Beauraing, *Imprimatur:* Namur, 16 juillet 1996 + J.M. Huet vic. épisc.

Kate Eschbach is a blogger, micro-influencer, speaker, photographer, and podcast host of *Tripping Over the Saints*—you can just call her a storyteller. She has been blogging since 2008 when she started a simple living scrapbook for her family after moving to the Arizona desert. She loves to create community and encourage others. She will tell anyone who stands still about the miracle that happened in her life. She is a Catholic convert, wife to her college sweetheart, and mom of five. You can find her at *SongsKateSang.com*.

X

MORNING STAR

Mary Is the Light That Leads Us Home

Kellie Gallegos

O sweet Mother of God,
I model my life on You;
You are for me the bright dawn:
In you I lose myself enraptured.

—Saint Faustina Kowalska (Diary, 1232)

My husband and I are campers, and I have found that I feel most in tune with God while sitting in the quiet of the night under the stars. When the noise of the world is silenced, I sense his love for me and witness his goodness. In the stillness, I see his self-revelation through his creation, and I am awestruck that the God of the universe calls me and desires me, even though I have so often been fickle.

My story is one of a journey away from the Church and back. I am a cradle Catholic from a devoted family. We did all the "right" Catholic things: we attended Mass every Sunday; my mom served as an extraordinary minister of the Eucharist; my Dad faithfully tithed; and I received all my sacraments. During the summer between eighth and ninth grade, while at a youth camp, I had an encounter that changed my relationship with God significantly. I met Jesus!

But as I entered high school, life became difficult. Besides the normal difficulties of adolescence, friendships, peer pressure, boys, and false opportunities for happiness, my mom became very ill with depression and tried to end her life. The attempt was not successful, but she continued to struggle with depression for all my high school years. She became emotionally disengaged from our life, and caring for our needs became a struggle. I was fueled by feelings of anger, loss, and betrayal. Our relationship with the Church also changed. I felt untethered, and I did not sense God.

I desperately tried to tether myself to all the wrong things. The noise in my head and heart became very loud. I became more argumentative with everyone and wrestled with my own inner thoughts. I turned to the world, instead of God, to silence the noise. When the worldly attempts did not order my pain, I searched even more frantically. My life looked disordered on the outside and felt more chaotic on the inside. I was holding onto my relationship with God by a thin thread, unable to hear his voice through the noise and pain. Eventually, I resolved that I needed to find God someplace other than the Catholic Church. And so, I left.

In my early twenties, I worked as a flight attendant and traveled around the world. I enjoyed the adventures, but the work also included many lonely days in hotel rooms. I read my Bible and periodically visited Catholic churches, but the longing for love persisted.

Somewhere along the way I began attending a non-denominational Protestant church. I got married, had two amazing boys, and got divorced. One thing that was consistent during these times was the inner chaos of my longings. I switched jobs often, moved several times, changed churches, and lived with unrest. Even while engaging in a relationship with God through the Protestant church, my adult life was marked by an unsettled soul. But through the changes, I held desperately to God, and his faithfulness followed me.

In 2010, I decided to return to school to get a degree in social work to become a therapist in mental health. A single mom at that time of two teenage boys, I needed a program that was online to accommodate the demands of my schedule. Surprisingly, the only school fully online, with flexible scheduling, was a Catholic university.

The first semester included mandatory theology classes. I began to hear of Mary as a "spiritual mother" and was very unsure what that meant. I was still a practicing Protestant, and denying a relationship with Mary was the one absolute that set Protestants apart from Catholics. I studied with great interest, seeking to justify why the Catholic Church's teachings were wrong. After all, hadn't they been the source of my alienation from God during those tumultuous years of Mom's illness? But the more I studied, the more I found those teachings were lights of truth illuminating my path.

Over the next thirteen years, the teachings of the Catholic Church continued to show up in my life, like stars shining in the dark. I remarried, and my husband was also a cradle Catholic who was attending a Protestant church. We began to seek God in our marriage. We were questioning so many things about our spiritual life, including our Protestant faith. We entered a season of spiritual unrest together but did not know where to find calm.

At some time during this period, I came across a Catholic podcast. I devoured every episode and reveled in the love expressed not only for God, but also for Mary. The hosts spoke of her with tenderness and honor. Never once did they elevate Mary over Jesus; but they loved her as a child loves her mother, and they recognized her as a model of faith for women. So different from what I had learned about Catholics' "Mary worship" in my Protestant church! I wanted to know Mary, to experience a motherly love that I still struggled to find in my earthly mother.

In December 2023, we moved my husband's aging parents close to us. The very first Sunday of January 2024 we offered to attend Mass with them at the Catholic church down the road from their new assisted living facility. As soon as we entered the church, a still, quiet peace enveloped me. During the Liturgy of the Eucharist, I felt a cool air on my skin. I turned to my husband and asked him if he felt it too. He nodded a yes.

The next week we returned to Mass with my in-laws. This time, as we knelt together during the Eucharistic prayer and Consecration, I sensed God. I sensed his presence. I felt the fulfillment of the longing that I had been searching for all those years. I began to weep. As I turned to look at my mother-in-law beside me, she too had tears streaming down her face. I elbowed my husband and exclaimed, "God is here!" In the presence of the body and blood of Jesus, I felt the Holy Spirit. I felt permission to surrender. I felt at home. We never returned to our Protestant church. I began to search for the answers to my questions in the *Catechism* and prayerfully asked Jesus to show me what he wants me to know about his mother.

The Litany of Loreto, approved by Pope Sixtus V in 1587, gives Mary the title "Morning Star."

The "morning star" is actually not a star at all, but the planet Venus. It shines brighter than any other star and appears in the sky before the break of dawn, just before the sun rises to a new day. Stars produce their own light, but planets do not. Venus's surface only reflects the light of the sun. This perfectly describes Mary's role, for as the Morning Star, she has no light of her own. She is a creature just like we are, but as the perfect, sinless creature, Mary perfectly reflects the glory of her Son.

St. John Henry Newman (1801–1890) wrote a series of reflections on the Litany of Loreto. He writes of Mary as the Morning Star,

> It is Mary's prerogative to be the *Morning* Star, which heralds in the sun. She does not shine for herself, or from herself, but she is the reflection of her and our Redeemer, and she glorifies Him. When she appears in the darkness, we know that He is close at hand. He is Alpha and Omega, the First and the Last, the Beginning and the End. Behold He comes quickly, and His reward is with Him, to render to everyone according to his works. "Surely I come quickly. Amen. Come, Lord Jesus."[1]

---

1 St. John Henry Newman, ed. Rev. W. P. Neville, "On the Assumption, (8) May 31," in *Meditations and Devotions* (London: Longmans, Green, & Co., 1907), https://www.newmanreader.org/works/meditations/meditations3.html.

St. John Paul II also wrote of Mary as the Morning Star is his encyclical *Redemptoris Mater* (Mother of the Redeemer). He describes Mary as

> the one who in the "night" of the Advent expectation began to shine like a true "Morning Star" (Stella Matutina). For just as this star, together with the "dawn," precedes the rising of the sun, so Mary from the time of her Immaculate Conception preceded the coming of the Savior, the rising of the "Sun of Justice" in the history of the human race.[2]

While researching and writing this chapter, I was camping with my husband. Sitting in the coolness of the dark, I wanted to witness the morning star. I looked up only to be met with heavy cloud cover and not a sliver of light. At first I felt disappointed, but then I thought how timely it was of God to allow me this experience while writing this chapter. Because, even though I could not see the illumination of the Morning Star, it does not mean that it was not there, offering a guiding light in the dark.

Isn't this always true? In the darkness of our disordered longings, there is a light. It's the light of a young girl who was willing to say yes to her part of the salvation story, "who in 'her pilgrimage of faith,' walked into the 'night of faith' sharing in the darkness of her son's suffering and death" bringing hope and salvation to the world. She was and still is the light that reflects and guides us to her Son.

For many years in the Protestant church, I accepted the teaching that I was a daughter of Eve. But when I came home to the Catholic Church, Jesus revealed to me his mother and showed me that I am also a daughter of Mary. She is our example of surrender, our example of a contemplative heart and what it means to live a life "full of grace" (Luke 1:28). "The Virgin Mary is the supreme model of faith" (CCC 273), and as our loving

---

2   St. John Paul II, *Redemptoris Mater*, March 25, 1987, https://www.vatican.va/content/john-paul-ii/en/encyclicals/documents/hf_jp-ii_enc_25031987_redemptoris-mater.html.

mother, she intercedes for us and shines forth for us with the glory of her Son, guiding us home.

Since returning home to the Church, my restless heart feels whole, and I have found "the peace of God, which passes all understanding" (Philippians 4:7). I am also learning to live a life that reflects being a daughter of Mary, one that is lived "full of grace." In doing so, I am working on grace and forgiveness for my earthly mom. It has been a "pilgrimage of faith," a journey of surrender to the nature of grace in Jesus, illuminated by Mary, the Morning Star, who helped me find my way home.

Kellie Gallegos is a psychotherapist passionate about helping women overcome shame to embrace their God-given purpose. She owns Unbelievable Grace Counseling & Therapy in Houston, TX, and is pursuing a master's degree in Catholic women and gender studies. A cradle Catholic who spent thirty-four years in the Protestant church, she shares her faith journey to inspire hope in others, especially those lost in their journey. She deeply values authenticity, healing, and God's unbelievable grace. Connect with Kellie at *kelliegallegos.com*

XI

OUR LADY OF THE ROSARY

The Chain That Binds Us to Jesus Through Mary

Marti Garcia

Some people are so foolish that they think they can go through life without the help of the Blessed Mother. Love the Madonna and pray the rosary, for her rosary is the weapon against the evils of the world today. All graces given by God pass through the Blessed Mother.

—St. Pio of Pietrelcina (Padre Pio)

As I sit here with my rosary in hand, a peace overcomes me like a hug from a dear old friend, one I have known far longer than I can remember. That dear friend, Mother Mary, has been a source of strength, love, guidance, and truth for me, since long before I even knew of her existence. Her intercession has been a stable pillar in my life.

My biological mother had a great devotion to Mary. I can remember being fidgety as a child during Mass, and my mother would give me her rosary to hold. The silver beads sparkled with such beauty, and I didn't want to let it go. My mom would also often drop me off at a community house of Benedictine nuns nearby for them to babysit me. I would sit on the back porch with them and make hosts, while they sang or recited prayers. I didn't know it then, but they were saying the Rosary. Even my birthday, October 7, shows the special care Mary has taken of me throughout my life. It is the feast day of Our Lady of the Rosary.

This feast day commemorates the victory of the Christian armada over the Turkish fleet in 1571. Pope St. Pius V called on the Church to pray the Rosary for the Christians to be victorious, even though they were a much smaller force. Thanks to the power of the Rosary, the Christians won the battle. In thanksgiving, the pope established the feast of Our Lady of Victory on the first Sunday of October. Pope St. Paul VI later moved the feast to October 7, "renaming it 'Our Lady of the Rosary' in order to remind the people of God how effective the Virgin Mary's prayers can be."[1]

There are numerous examples of the power of the Rosary throughout the centuries. The Order of Preachers, founded by St. Dominic in the thirteenth century, has a special devotion to the Rosary and actively promotes it. The friars share the following story about St. Dominic, which shows how powerful and important the Rosary is:

> Saint Dominic learned this truth almost 800 years ago, when the Blessed Virgin Mary appeared to him in a vision. Aware of his distress at being unable to convert more Albigensians back to Catholicism, the Blessed Mother spoke to Dominic and offered these words of wisdom: "Wonder not that you have obtained so little fruit by your labors, for you have spent them on barren soil, not yet watered with the dew of Divine grace. When God willed to renew the face of the earth, He began by sending down on it the fertilizing rain of the angelic salutation. Therefore, preach my psalter composed of 150 angelic salutations and 15 Our Fathers, and you will obtain an abundant harvest."[2]

---

1 Dominican Friars, Province of the Most Holy Name of Jesus, "Our Lady of the Rosary," https:// opwest.org/olr.

2 Ibid.

Hundreds of years after St. Dominic, Venerable Fr. Patrick Peyton famously promoted the Rosary in the twentieth century. He was such a zealous soldier for Mary and her Rosary that he was known as the Rosary Priest. Coming from a devout family that prayed the Rosary every night, his sole purpose when he became a priest was to encourage devotion to Mary and the Rosary. He utilized all the media platforms of the 1960s,'70s, and '80s to share his love for the Rosary, and he also organized events like the 540 Rosary Rallies. He created a program that allowed any volunteer to make rosaries, which were then shipped to various locations worldwide. For many years, I partook of this great program. I felt my hands could plant the seeds to help Mary. I would pray over each one as I strung the beads that formed the rosary. As founder of the Holy Cross Family Ministries, this rosary ministry still exists today, and the faithful can also visit the Fr. Peyton Center and Museum of Prayer in North Easton, MA.[3]

Have you ever thought about the intricate making of such a beautiful gift from Mary? People have answered the call to create rosaries all for Mary on her mission to bring people closer to Jesus through the Rosary. I am drawn to the makings of a beautiful rosary. Somehow my prayers feel extra special. Rosaries come in a wide variety of shapes, sizes, and colors. From the ornate to the simple plastic ones, they each carry a request from Mother Mary: Pray.

A dear friend of mine is writing a book about a World War II soldier who was a prisoner of war, and he told me a particularly powerful story that shows how a specially made rosary can affect a person's life. As he was interviewing the grandson, who is still alive, they began discussing how his grandfather would carry a "pull chain" rosary (the name was taken from the pull chain on servicemens' dog tags). The grandson shared how important the Rosary was for his grandfather as a support and protection.

---

3 The Father Peyton Center, Holy Cross Family Ministries, https://www.hcfm.org/father-peyton-center

Imagine finding a rosary that is over a hundred years old! Many rosaries are passed down through generations within families. I feel something special when I pray using my mother's shiny silver rosary from when I was little—my hand over hers as I pray each decade.

My closeness to Mary and the Rosary has sustained me through many difficult moments over the years, adding to my sense of strength. In some situations, I have felt so helpless that I would just walk around holding my rosary and saying, "Mary, please help." I have kept a rosary under my pillow since I can remember to pray with on those nights when I toss and turn and can't get to sleep. I have learned from personal experience that the Rosary remains a steadfast ally in our daily spiritual battle.

Today I reflect on who I am and who I have become because of my love for the Rosary.

I wasn't fortunate enough to be given the name Mary. My older sister was given that name. I was given Martha. For so many years, whenever the gospel story about Mary and Martha was read, my sister never failed to remind me that she was the good one. I smile now, knowing that I have the best of both names. Mary is the "heart of my heart," and Martha is who I have become. The name Martha is associated with qualities such as reliability, determination, kindness, and a sense of strength, with a bit of anxiety added in. That sums up me: the heart of Mary, with the determination of Martha. And the Rosary helps me keep these two things in balance.

Pope Leo XIII loved the Rosary so much that he has been called the Pope of the Rosary. He wrote twelve encyclicals on this powerful prayer and the Blessed Virgin Mary. In his encyclical *Octobri Mense* (1891), he offers the following encouragement to all the faithful to pray the Rosary:

> Now, among the several rites and manners of paying honor to the Blessed Mary, some are to be preferred, inasmuch as we know them to be most powerful and most pleasing to our Mother; and for this reason, we specially mention by name and recommend the Rosary. The common language has given the name of corona to this manner

of prayer, which recalls to our minds the great mysteries of Jesus and Mary united in joys, sorrows, and triumphs. The contemplation of these august mysteries, contemplated in their order, affords to faithful souls a wonderful confirmation of faith, protection against the disease of error, and increase of the strength of the soul. The soul and memory of him who thus prays, enlightened by faith, are drawn towards these mysteries by the sweetest devotion, are absorbed therein, and are surprised before the work of the Redemption of mankind, achieved at such a price and by events so great. The soul is filled with gratitude and love before these proofs of Divine love; its hope becomes enlarged, and its desire is increased for those things which Christ has prepared for such as have united themselves to Him in imitation of His example and in participation in His sufferings. The prayer is composed of words proceeding from God Himself, from the Archangel Gabriel, and from the Church; full of praise and of high desires; and it is renewed and continued in an order at once fixed and various; its fruits are ever new and sweet.[4]

Saint Josemaría Escrivá said, "If you say the Holy Rosary every day, with a spirit of faith and love, our Lady will make sure she leads you very far along her Son's path."[5]

As an adult, I recall a time when the fruits of my Rosary prayers opened me up to the beautiful love of Mary and allowed her to teach me where her love always seeks to lead us. This was a time when I was being led into a deeper faith and prayer life. I was deep in prayer during Eucharistic adoration, preparing to attend a women's retreat. Many women were kneeling around me, praying. My prayer was directed to Mary, praising her as my mother and the Mother of God. Then, in my mind's eye, I looked up and saw Mary. She looked straight into my eyes. She slowly shook her head from side to side in a signal of "no." Gently grabbing my left elbow and lifting me up to a standing position, she pointed to her

---

4 Pope Leo XIII, *Octobri Mense* (on the Rosary), September 22, 1891, https://www.vatican.va/content/leo-xiii/en/encyclicals/documents/hf_l-xiii_enc_22091891_octobri-mense.html.

5 St. Josemaría Escrivá, *Furrow*, no. 691.

left. I stood and followed her pointing finger to the appearance of Jesus descending, seated on a throne. I then realized what she was teaching me: her Son Jesus deserves the utmost adoration and praise. Mary's love and intercession purify our prayers and actions as she presents them to the Lord.

Mary is always attentive when we ask for her help, but she especially loves the Rosary. I recently read that she gives special attention to our petitions when we pray the Rosary on October 7. I don't know if this is true, but I love to think about it, since this is my feast day too—Our Lady of the Rosary. On my birthday every year, I get to feast on the unceasing love of Mary and her intercession.

No matter what the date is, we can be confident that we are walking side by side with all the saints and angels when we hold our rosaries tightly and pray together to change the world into a better place.

Our Lady of the Rosary, pray for us.

Marti Garcia's spiritual life began with the Rosary. A published author, she especially treasures being able to share the gifts God has given her through service in her local parish. You can learn more about her and find the encyclicals of Pope Leo XIII on the Rosary, articles on Fr. Peyton and his ministers, information about the Legion of Mary, and Rosary resources at *martigarcia.org*.

XII

OUR LADY OF FATIMA

How Mary Teaches Us to Pay Attention to the Details

Margaret Gartlgruber

You have hidden these things from the wise and the
intelligent and have revealed them to infants.

—Matthew 11:25

Last night, I brushed my teeth with Preparation-H. The tube of hemorrhoid cream was right next to the sample toothpaste the dentist gives after checkups. It had been a long day and a long drive to my friend's house in Maryland, and I was tired. But I had gotten prosciutto stuck in my teeth and could not wait to brush them and go to sleep. As I finished brushing (yes, I had fully brushed!) I thought, "This is the worst tasting toothpaste ever!"

Then I looked.

Humiliated, grossed out, and hoping I had not just poisoned myself, I immediately began paying the consequence of my lack of attention. Brushing my teeth (with actual toothpaste this time) again and again and again, I beat myself up for being such a ditz. What was wrong with me? Flossing and flossing again, trying to get the taste out, I could almost hear Jesus saying to me what he told his followers: "Pay attention" (Mark 4:24).

This sparked a memory from a few weeks before of an unusual experience in confession. There is a shrine near my home in rural New Jersey that I tend to take for granted. Set in the farmlands with beautiful views of the mountains all around, the National Blue Army Shrine of Our Lady of Fatima is a pilgrimage site dedicated to spreading the message of Fatima. Consequently, many here have a particular devotion to Our Lady of Fatima, including the priest I was seeing for confession on this day.

I entered the confessional in a troubled state and immediately began weeping. The priest, barely able to understand my confession, saw my heart, explained some of my sins, and then told me, "Satan is real and at work. Sr. Lucia said the final battle between Christ and Satan would be over marriage and the family."[1] This idea shook me. Was I that distracted in my own sorrow that I had forgotten about Satan? Wasn't Lucia one of the Fatima children? And when had she said that?

When I left the confessional, I knelt in front of a tableau of Mary, dressed in beautiful white splendor, arms outstretched before three children in a serene countryside setting. Gazing at this image as I had a hundred times before, it occurred to me how little I knew about any of the three children of Fatima. I knew the basic facts: Mary visited three children each month for six months. She showed them visions, gave them messages and instructions, and then, in October 1917, the great Miracle of the Sun occurred. But these facts had never resonated in my heart.

Ashamed, I realized that I had been minimizing what happened, thinking, "Aww. Lucky children, getting a visit from Mary, isn't that sweet?" I mean, who pays attention to children other than to notice how cute they are (or maybe how ill-behaved)? As parents we clothe them,

---

1   Lucia wrote to Cardinal Carlo Caffarra in a handwritten note (1983): "A decisive battle between the kingdom of Christ and Satan will be over marriage and the family, those who work for the good of the family will experience persecution and tribulation. But do not be afraid, Our Lady has already crushed his head." See "Fatima visionary predicted 'final battle' would be over marriage, family," CNA, October 13, 2021, https://www.catholicnewsagency.com/news/34155/fatima-visionary-predicted-final-battle-would-be-over-marriage-family.

feed them, teach them, care for them. But how often do we dismiss them, thinking, "What could they know about life?" So after that confession, where the priest advised me using Lucia's own words, I told myself I needed to get more details. But I hadn't done it.

Now, at my friend's bathroom sink, as I rinsed yet again, trying to get the horrid taste out of my mouth, I thought, "Maybe the devil really is in the details." The small details may be worth a closer look.

Imagine living in Portugal in 1917. World War I is in full swing—men going off to war or worried about going off to war or coming back wounded or not at all. The Freemasons were in charge and determined to eradicate Catholicism. New ideologies were seducing nations. And yet, the sheep still needed shepherds. A small thing. Often, as in the case of the three Fatima visionaries, children were left in charge of this job. Through these small children tending sheep, God communicated an important message to the world, first through the visit of an angel and then through Mary.

Lucia, the oldest at ten years old, loved playing games, going to festivals, and dancing. She attracted children to her like a magnet. The constantly surrounded her, among them her cousin, Jacinta, a sweet child of six. Headstrong and curious, she loved to play games as long as they were her favorites—games she would win. If this did not happen, she would go off in a corner and pout until she got her way. Jacinta's older brother, Francisco, seven years old, was the opposite. Everything slid off him without a care. He liked playing but did not mind which games, as he was content with losing. The three children played together while they tended the sheep, hurrying through their prayers so they could have more time for games. Until the day the Angel of Peace came, when everything changed.

The angel visited them three times, teaching them to pray and worship, encouraging them to make sacrifices, and finally offering them Communion. He told them, "Make everything you do a sacrifice, offer it to God as an act of reparation for the sins by which He is offended, and in supplication for the conversion of sinners."[2] This was all to prepare them for something greater.

A year later, on May 13, 1917, a lady in white appeared to the three children, saying only that she was "of heaven." She instructed them about many things over the next six visits, and also granted them visions, which had the greatest impact on the children.

In one of these visions, Mary showed the children her Immaculate Heart. Lucia remembers:

> Our Lady opened her hands . . .to us a light so intense . . .it penetrated our hearts and the innermost depths of our souls, making us see ourselves in God, who was that light, more clearly than we see ourselves in the best of mirrors. In front of the palm of Our Lady's right hand was a Heart encircled by thorns which pierced it. We understood that this was the Immaculate Heart of Mary outraged by the sins of humanity, and seeking reparation.

This image of Mary's Immaculate Heart captivated me. *Immaculate* means perfectly clean, spotless. Just as the Ark of the Covenant of Moses was made perfectly clean, Mary, created by God, himself, also made perfectly clean, as she must, in order to hold the ark of the new covenant—Jesus. This includes her heart—a heart that held so much, as we read in the Gospel of Luke that Mary kept all these things in her heart. Through her perfect heart she penetrates our hearts, reflecting the love God has for us. The light of God is too bright for man to look at, but through Mary we can see it, and in that light, we can see his love for us.

Many images of Mary's Immaculate Heart include the sword (or swords) of sorrow. But in this vision, the children recall seeing a heart with only thorns, no sword. I had never noticed or even considered the thorns surrounding Mary's heart before. I had always focused only on the sword, not paying attention again. I immediately recalled my tears

---

2   Sister Lucia, *Fatima in Lucia's Own Words: The Memoirs of Sister Lucia, the Last Fatima Visionary* (KIC, 2015), 195, Kindle Location 2798.

in the confessional. None of my tears were because of a big thing or a sword, but rather a great many small things added together—thorns in my own heart.

We all have these thorns. We try to ignore them. We have to in order to run our families or simply go about our daily lives. But there they sit, unknown to all, adding up. Sometimes those little pricks add up into some major chest pain. My friend Theresa had one such experience. Certain she was having a heart attack, she rushed to the ER. The medical staff found nothing. "Anxiety" they called it. "Thorns." That is what they should have called it.

The small thorns can take their toll if we do not pay attention to them, taking us away from God and stealing our peace. The circle of thorns around Mary's heart and the crown of thorns on Jesus—these thorns represent our sin. These sins hurt them, just as the thorns in our own hearts hurt us.

In a later, terrifying vision, Mary showed the three children hell. No one likes to talk about hell, especially with children, yet God did not hesitate to show them the truth. "The rays of light seemed to penetrate the earth and we saw as if it were a sea of fire. Plunged in this fire were demons and souls in human form, like transparent burning embers, all blackened or burnished bronze, floating about."[3]

Then Mary told them, "You have seen hell, where poor sinners go. To save them, God wishes to establish in the world devotion to My Immaculate Heart. . . . I shall come to ask for the Communion of Reparation on the First Saturdays.[4]

She then went on to urge them, "Pray, pray very much and make sacrifices for sinners; for many souls go to hell, because there are none to sacrifice themselves and to pray for them."[5]

---

3   Ibid., 204, Kindle edition Location 2923.
4   Ibid., 205, Kindle edition Location 2930.
5   Ibid., 207, Kindle edition Location 2958.

After seeing Mary's perfect heart jabbed with the thorns of mankind's sins, the children experienced this vision of the consequence of those sins: hell. So often we think of sin as only being very big things, but in reality, it is also all the little things, the distractions. The thorns. It is the small things that make us forget who we are and where we want to spend eternity.

The children's response to these messages reminds me of a game my kids played when they were little, called "Would You Rather. . ." There would be a question asked, such as, "Would you rather eat a rotten tomato or an overripe banana?" Or "Would you rather lose your arms or your legs?"

The Fatima children asked, *Would you rather console God or offer up sacrifices for sinners?* Francisco saw God's sadness and wanted only to console him, often skipping school to pray to the hidden Jesus in the tabernacle. Jacinta, on the other hand, most affected by the vision of hell, began sacrificing for sinners: giving up play time to pray, then giving her lunch to poor children, eventually seeking all kinds of ways to be uncomfortable, until finally embracing a long illness. Both children died within two years of Mary's visits after much suffering.

Lucia faced a different question: *Would you rather lie if it means having the love of your family, or stay silent and suffer endless questioning, doubts, and interrogation for love of God?* Lucia chose the latter, even though it meant facing her mother's accusations of lying and subsequent manipulations to force her to recant, and being constantly persecuted and questioned. She was the only one of the children to live a long life in order to spread the message, suffering much in order to do so.

Lucia, a few years later in her convent cell, finally received the instructions Mary promised in 1917 in order to bring about the devotion to her Immaculate Heart. Jesus came with Mary this time expressing sadness at how blasphemed and dishonored his mother is. Lucia was then asked to spread the five First Saturdays devotion. Mary promises special graces and assistance at the hour of death for those who faithfully do the following on five consecutive first Saturdays:

- Go to confession within eight days before or after the first Saturday.
- Receive Communion.
- Pray five decades of the Rosary.
- In addition to the five decades, spend fifteen minutes in meditation on any of the mysteries of the Rosary.
- State the intention to make reparation for offenses against Mary's Immaculate Heart.

Small things can have a big impact. Small thorns in our hearts can add up into anxiety, tears, and despair as I experienced in confession. Yet it works the other way, too. Small children can hear and deliver big messages. Small sacrifices can console Jesus and convert sinners, keeping them from hell.

Our response, therefore, should be to pay attention to prayer and penance. Pray a lot, especially the Rosary. Practice the Five First Saturdays devotion. And each and every day, pay attention to the distractions threatening to take our focus off Jesus and heaven. Pay attention to all the opportunities that come our way to offer penance for the conversion of sinners. Every ache, pain, complaint—all of these small offerings can have an eternal impact. Even, I hope, brushing your teeth with hemorrhoid cream.

Margaret Gartlgruber wants moms to know the importance of their call to motherhood and how much they are loved by God! Sharing her experiences raising kids as a Catholic mom in a public school world, Margaret encourages moms to grow in virtue while fully embracing their vocations with joy. Get a copy of the Fatima prayers, devotion, and a bonus "15 Simple Morning Prayers" at *ruledbybananas.com*

XIII

MARY HELP OF CHRISTIANS

How Our Lady Always Leads Us to Jesus

Rose Ann Heisel

When Jesus saw his mother and the disciple
whom he loved standing beside her, he said to
his mother, "Woman, behold your son."

—John 19:26

In 2023, I was on my second pilgrimage to the Basilica and National Shrine of Mary Help of Christians, located in Hubertus, Wisconsin. The bus left St. Michael, Minnesota, before sunrise. My thoughts were focused on peaceful moments of silence, prayer, and worship on familiar church grounds.

Once we reached the shrine and disembarked, I was first drawn to a beautiful white statue of St. Thérèse of Lisieux, one of my favorite saints. That day, I wore a necklace that contained a third-class relic of St. Thérèse. Later, after Mass, it felt like her guiding hand was leading me toward the Shrine Chapel off the sanctuary in the church. I noticed crutches of all sizes at the entrance of the chapel. I later found out they were left behind by people who came to Our Lady for healing.

The Shrine Chapel displays a rare statue of Mary, depicting her as a young mother offering her Son to all who pray in this chapel. I was fascinated by how the statue of Mary came into the chapel, as the Shrine's website relates:

> In 1878, eighteen young barefoot women, dressed in white robes with blue ribbons, carried the statue to the top of Holy Hill. The women were escorted by an entourage of 100 men on horseback, many priests and delegates from all over the state. These dedicated pilgrims filled the air with songs and prayers as they processed to their goal.[1]

Since then, many individuals have reported miracles and healings from praying in this spot. I wondered what was in store for me in this chapel.

The chapel felt holy and comfortable, like a warm blanket was draped over my shoulders. Silence and peace encapsulated the space. An interior calm came over me. A stillness pressed over my body, so I could not move. I no longer could hold on to my own thoughts. The chapel took on a different lighting. Something was taking place, and my life going forward would take on a new meaning.

It seemed as if the chapel became flooded with a heavenly gold light that appeared to shower dazzling gold stars around me. It reminded me of Revelation 12:1, "A great portent appeared in heaven: a woman clothed with the sun, with the moon beneath her feet, and on her head a crown of twelve stars." The room seemed to have no walls, and the statue of Mary and Jesus became larger and appeared to be closer in front of me. My eyes were fixed on Mary and Jesus, and I could not turn my head. Mary's light alone engulfed the entire chapel. I felt as if I was being taken out of myself into a supernatural realm. I wondered if I was seeing heaven.

Shortly before this trip to Holy Hill, I had consecrated myself to Mary and asked her to make my interior life like hers so I could have a deeper relationship with her Son. Now, I believe Mary was giving me her answer.

---

1 Holy Hill, "Shrine Chapel," https://www.holyhill.com/basilica/shrine-of-mary-help-of-christians.

There was a great silence in the chapel. Then Mary brought Jesus to me. It was like she was presenting her Son to me, as if to say, "Here is my Son, whom I will give to you, whom I love with my whole heart and soul."

I felt Mary's powerful love as our mother. She continues to draw Christians toward her Son. I reflected on the significance of Christ's words from the Cross: "Here is your mother" (John 19:27). My heart melted into tears. I am not sure if I was breathing at this point. I knew that I had just had a heavenly experience.

I thought of Jesus during the Transfiguration and the words that God the Father said to the three apostles who witnessed it: "This is my Son, the Beloved; with him I am well pleased; listen to him" (Matthew 17:5).

Then I saw Jesus come forward, holding an ornate gold book of the gospels. Jesus was so much brighter than his mother, but I could still see him well. He appeared to be twelve years old, the age he had been when he stayed behind in Jerusalem to teach in the Temple (see Luke 2:41–51).

I felt drawn deeper into the heart of Jesus, and I understood that to be a disciple of Jesus is to take Mary his mother into our own hearts, and to abandon all to her presence, her care, and her love.

So it is no surprise that in my encounter on Holy Hill, Mary placed herself in a loving manner off to the side. Mary, who was full of grace and the Holy Spirit, was bringing Jesus Christ into my presence. I felt love pouring over me. I saw her only in my peripheral vision. Jesus was at the center. I was so overwhelmed with joy, I asked Jesus "What does this mean? What am I being called to do?" But I heard no reply, and the vision ended. I reflected for a moment on words from St. John of the Cross: "The Father spoke one Word, which was his Son, and this Word he speaks always in eternal silence, and in silence must it be heard by the soul."[2]

If we do not hear the answers to our questions, perhaps God is inviting us to search him out more deeply in prayer. We can do this by making it a point to find more quiet moments to talk to God with attention and

---

2   St. John of the Cross, *Sayings of Light and Love*, #100.

focus. This is what he wants from us: an intimate relationship. We can make space for this encounter by creating a special prayer space in our home and inviting him to sit with us there each day. He must always be foremost in our minds.

After my time in prayer in the chapel ended, I decided to finish my pilgrimage at the basilica's gift store. I wanted to purchase an icon in remembrance of the statue in the chapel and my life-changing encounter with Mary and Jesus that showed me my new ministry.

After that pilgrimage to Holy Hill, I began to create retreats to gather people together with a focus on how Mary brings help to Christians by leading us to her Son. My devotion to Mary has grown deeper, and the spirit of Advent is always present in my heart. Now the joyful mysteries of the Rosary bring back memories of my supernatural encounter in the chapel. The icon still sits on my desk, and daily I reflect on this spiritual encounter with Jesus.

As I stepped outside into the cool October breeze, I once again put my hand on my St. Thérèse medal. To my surprise, I saw white rose petals scattered all over the ground. Everyone else was walking by them as if they were old fallen leaves. But I started following the path of rose petals, which led me back to the statue of St. Thérèse.

I felt little Thérèse encouraging me to go back one more time to the chapel and read the entire copper plaque on the wall. I did so, and I was surprised to read that visions are possible in this chapel. Now I can share my story that the Lord has done great things for me.

RoseAnn Heisel is a published writer who enjoys poetry and art. She writes to share the gifts and insights she has received over the years, offering readers a path to deeper intimacy with God. She also leads small groups, organizes retreats, and evangelizes in quiet ways inspired by her favorite saints. She can be reached at *roseannheisel@aol.com.*

XIV

OUR LADY OF PERPETUAL HELP

How Mary's Powerful Intercession Carries Us

Barb Lishko

*"For nothing will be impossible with God." Then
Mary said, "Here am I, the servant of the Lord;
let it be with me according to your word."*

—Luke 1:37–38

One morning when I was eight years old, my father woke up and quickly realized that his body was paralyzed from his waist to his toes. I watched as the ambulance took him away. He would not return for several months, and he never walked again.

Prayer, which had always been an important part of our family's life, became a vital source of peace and strength for all of us. We had an image of Our Lady of Perpetual Help hanging in our home, and we always gathered around it to pray the Rosary. This early experience of an active, living faith became the foundation on which my faith and trust in God grew.

When I was a child, I was a little afraid of the image of Our Lady of Perpetual Help. Her piercing eyes and unsmiling lips seemed disapproving. For a long time, I had little knowledge about Mary other than the Rosary, this image, and the Christmas manger scene.

Becoming a wife and mother helped me begin to fall in love with Our Lady of Perpetual Help. In motherhood, its joys and sorrows, I realized that we shared a common bond and purpose—except, while I only worried about five children, Mary's motherhood encompassed all of humanity. In my trials and faced with the unpredictable nature of human freedom, I prayed to her, seeking wisdom and guidance.

Despite being a mother myself, I found peace knowing I was also her daughter. I had my heavenly mother ever available and attentive to my struggles, pain, and confusion. What a relief to know that I didn't need to figure it all out or have all the answers. She was my advocate and intercessor *par excellence*, the tender mother on whom I could always rely. With each tiny miracle my confidence grew in her intercessory power and tender compassion.

My curiosity about the icon of Our Lady drew me to find out more about its history and significance.

The Byzantine Icon of Our Lady of Perpetual Help is thought to date from the fourteenth or fifteenth century. The artist remains anonymous but may have been a monk.

Around 1495, a wine merchant stole the image from a monastery in Crete and brought it into his home in Rome. Later, on his deathbed, the merchant asked his friend to take it to a church for public veneration. Instead, his friend held onto it. Our Lady appeared to his young daughter in a dream, requesting that the image be venerated in the Church of St. Matthew, which was located between the Basilicas of St. Mary Major and St. John Lateran. The image was moved to the church, and it became known as "The Madonna of Saint Matthew." Countless faithful pilgrims traveled there for three hundred years, and abundant graces flowed upon those who invoked Mary's intercession.[1]

Many miracles were recorded and attributed to Mary's intercession as Our Lady of Perpetual Help. Sadly, after Napoleon's troops invaded Rome,

---

1 "What is the story behind the image of Our Lady of Perpetual Help?" Catholic Straight Answers, https://catholicstraightanswers.com/what-is-the-story-behind-the-image-of-our-lady-of-perpetual-help/.

St. Matthew's was destroyed. The icon was saved and moved to St. Mary's in Posterula, where it remained for forty years and was nearly forgotten. By divine providence, it was rediscovered and moved to the Church of St. Alphonsus, where it continues to be displayed and venerated.

As a young woman, I came to the conclusion that if God Almighty entrusted his son Jesus to her motherly care, then I must entrust myself to her as well. I begged for her assistance in finding my future husband. I offered her a deal: I would pray the Rosary each night, and she would help me find the man I was to marry. After working my shift at the hospital, I'd drive to our parish and sit in the dark parking lot, praying. Months later, in the most unlikely place—a disco—my prayers were answered. My husband and I have now been married for over forty-five years.

Early in our marriage, we had difficulty conceiving after a miscarriage. I knew that I needed my heavenly Mother and her intercession once again. For years, we persisted in prayer while God was putting everything in motion (unbeknownst to us).

My husband was a pilot in the U.S. Air Force, and we were stationed for a time in England. The stress of the move, lack of housing, and failure to achieve a pregnancy weighed heavily on my heart and mind. Still, I persisted in prayer, asking Our Lady for guidance and help.

A year into our tour, we received a letter from my parents, requesting to visit. They not only wanted to see us but to travel to Lourdes, France. My father was not the only one who wanted a miracle.

Lourdes was peaceful, and we spent three incredibly prayerful days there. We took in the baths, joined the rosary procession each evening, and joyfully pushed my father in his wheelchair up the precarious Stations of the Cross. Through it all, Mother Mary was refreshing my soul. Lourdes was proof that miracles happen every day through Mary's loving intercession.

We spent the next few weeks traveling with my parents through Europe.

Nine months after our pilgrimage to Lourdes, our son was born. Mary had come through again.

As the years passed, we continued to rely on Our Lady of Perpetual Help, as we added to our family and were blessed with two more sons and two daughters. We taught our children how to pray the Rosary and to entrust themselves to their heavenly Mother. Our babies grew and became teens saddled with changing emotions and peculiar personalities that accompany puberty. Outside pressure from friends, culture, and the desire to fit in created strangers in our household.

I offered countless hours of fervent prayer, far more than when they were little and safely tucked in their beds at night. Now they were mobile, independent, and growing cynical in the polluted environment of high school and college life. Their challenges were pressing and more complicated. We attended Mass regularly as a family, but it still felt like they were hanging on by a thread. Every night, I would drench the beads with tears, praying our heavenly Mother would intercede and protect them.

There were times when each child wandered off-track. Thankfully, they had been firmly grounded in the truth of Catholicism and able to eventually recognize counterfeits and lies. God was at work, and our prayers continued. His plans for each child would be realized in his time and way.

Ultimately, Our Lady of Perpetual Help guided them all home as, one by one, they met the spouses ordained for them and married in the Church. They continue to practice the Catholic faith, teaching their children the prayers and practices so deeply planted in their hearts long ago. The joy this brings us as parents and grandparents is immeasurable.

Within a couple of years, our sweet grandbabies will enter the crazy years of puberty. Thankfully, they will be fortified and equipped with the same tools their parents and grandparents have used: fervent and trusting devotion to Mary.

Why is the Blessed Virgin so powerful in the raging spiritual battle for souls? The *Catechism* teaches:

> This motherhood of Mary in the order of grace continues uninter-
> ruptedly from the consent which she loyally gave at the Annunciation

and which she sustained without wavering beneath the Cross, until the eternal fulfilment of all the elect. Taken up to heaven, she did not lay aside this saving office but by her manifold intercession continues to bring us the gifts of eternal salvation. . . . Therefore, the Blessed Virgin is invoked in the Church under the titles of Advocate, Helper, Benefactress, and Mediatrix. (CCC 969)

Never worry that going to Mary may offend Jesus. It was God's plan for Christ to come into the world through her, and desired that he be raised and influenced by her maternal love and care. Thus St. Maximilian Kolbe counsels, "Never be afraid of loving the Blessed Virgin too much. You can never love her more than Jesus did."

The icon of our Lady of Perpetual Help aids us in understanding what the Church has always taught and believed about Mary's powerful intercession. Icons are written in a spirit of penance and prayer, and they make present what they represent. They are windows into heaven and points of encounter between the mystery of God and man.

Throughout history, this icon was known by two titles: Virgin of the Passion and Our Lady of Perpetual Help. The Virgin Mary peers out at us as we implore her help. She inclines her head gently toward her son, whom she tenderly holds. The Greek letters on either side of the top proclaim her as Mother of God. The name Jesus Christ is written to his right. Two angels on either side hold the instruments of Christ's Passion—St. Michael on the left and St. Gabriel on the right. It is as if the boy Jesus saw these instruments of his torture and ran to his Mother in haste to be consoled. He has lost one sandal, exposing the sole of his foot, which symbolizes his human nature.

This icon reminds us that God is always close, and that Christ took on the suffering that should have been ours, willingly carrying his Cross and thus giving meaning and value to our suffering. Mother Mary never left his side through his agony, and her loving intercession is always available to those who ask.

As a child, before I had experienced the cross of suffering, I could not understand that Mary's eyes in the icon portray deep sadness at the suffering she and her Son would endure for love of us. Her tiny mouth represents not disapproval, but her perfect humility.

Now, after a lifetime of carrying heavy crosses, especially as a mother, I recognize that Mary's eyes share deeply in my sorrow and pain. She understands in a way that only one who has been there can. In the midst of our most painful trials, God had a plan for good. As St. Paul reminds us, "We know that all things work together for good for those who love God, who are called according to his purpose" (Romans 8:28).

Sometimes, in God's Providence, we are not granted the miracle we seek. While my father did not receive the miracle he hoped for, his daughter did.

We can become bitter when things don't work out as we think they should, or we can choose to surrender and trust God. Mary's intercession and continual graces fortified my dad for the cross which he would carry for the rest of his life. His witness to the power of redemptive suffering impacted countless people. Sometimes the gift we receive is not readily apparent or visible. We must always trust that God knows best.

Our crosses don't always make sense to us now. Our Lady can help open our hearts and minds to the blessings God wants to give us through our suffering. She has been there and her example of surrender and complete cooperation with the Father's will is invaluable.

Our Lady of Perpetual Help, pray for us.

Barbara Lishko cooked her way into full-time Church ministry for over twenty years. *"If you feed them, they will come"* describes her approach to ministry: Food has been the catalyst, faith the main course. Barbara shares the wild adventure of married life with Mark, a deacon. Their five children have produced a fruitful harvest of eighteen grandkids. Read her reflections at *BarbLishko.com*.

XV

MARY, MOTHER OF THE EUCHARIST

How Our Lady Teaches Us to Receive, Believe, and Adore

Julianne Jackson

> *Mary, give me your Heart: so beautiful, so pure,*
> *so immaculate; your Heart so full of love and*
> *humility that I may be able to receive Jesus in the*
> *Bread of Life and love Him as you love Him.*[1]

—St. Teresa of Calcutta

Many years ago, I happened upon an outdoor garden shop and decided to stop in, as I needed a concrete bench. As I browsed, something colorful at the far end of the yard overgrown with weeds caught my eye. Seeing me move in that direction to investigate, the owner of the shop came up behind me and said, "Ma'am, that is our trash pile." Something drew me to keep walking. If ever there was a drum roll from heaven, it was at this moment.

As I reached the spot, I bent down and saw a discarded statue of Jesus. He was intact but childishly painted. One unusually large hand was

---

1   St. Teresa of Calcutta, "Mother Teresa's Prayer to Mary," https://mycatholicprayers.com/prayers/mother-teresas-prayer-to-mary/.

pointing to his exposed heart, his eyes intent. It seemed like an invitation. Something stirred within me and my heart skipped a beat. I blurted out, "I want this statue."

The lady replied, "That is the garbage pile. No one is interested in a Sacred Heart of Jesus statue. Come over here and I will show you some angels."

"How much is it?" I asked.

The lady replied, "It is poor quality and not for sale."

"I'll take it," I said and quickly reached into my purse and handed her a fistful of bills.

As I walked away cradling the statue in my arms, I could hear her say, "Why would anyone care about the Sacred Heart of Jesus?"

Tears began to well up in my eyes from hearing her remark. As I carefully placed the statue of Jesus in the passenger side of my car and belted him in, I fervently uttered a simple prayer: "Mama Mary, bring me into the Heart of Jesus."

At the Last Supper Jesus, burning with the desire to be one with his apostles, instituted the Eucharist, thus giving us his heart for all ages. Devotion to his heart and Eucharistic devotion cannot be separated. St. Peter Julian Eymard, founder of the Blessed Sacrament Fathers, writes, "Let then this living and pulsating Heart be the center of our life. Let us learn to honor the Sacred Heart in the Eucharist. Let us never separate the Sacred Heart from the Eucharist." To know Jesus' heart, we go to Mother Mary. Eymard continues, "Where on earth shall we find Jesus but in the arms of Mary? Was it not her who gave us the Eucharist?"[2] Indeed, who else is so close to his Sacred Heart? For the nine months Mary carried Jesus in her womb, their hearts beat in sync.

In his 2003 encyclical letter *Ecclesia de Eucharistia*, St. John Paul II writes, "If the Church and the Eucharist are inseparably united, the

---

2   St. Peter Julian Eymard, *Our Lady of the Blessed Sacrament Vol.7* (Emmanuel Publications), 1.

same ought to be said of Mary and the Eucharist."[3] He continues, "Mary can guide us towards this most holy sacrament, because she herself has a profound relationship with it."[4] Mary, the Mother of Jesus, the Mother of the Eucharist, longs to give her Son's heart to the world as she first did over two thousand years ago. She wants to teach us how to live a Eucharistic life.

John Paul II refers to Mary as the "woman of the Eucharist" and writes, "The church which looks to Mary as a model, is also called to imitate her in her relationship with this most holy mystery."[5] Pondering Mary's life, we can learn how she lived Eucharistic faith well before Jesus instituted the Eucharist, and she can show us how to be Eucharistic people. Mary, Mother of the Eucharist, can teach us how to receive, believe, and adore.

To receive means to accept from the giver that which is not of us. To receive from God, we must first recognize our need to receive and open our hearts. At the Annunciation, Mary received God's grace through the power of the Holy Spirit, and with that she received the gift of her Son, body, blood, soul, and divinity, in her very self. Jesus was conceived, made incarnate, through Mary's receiving.

Of course, Mary was full of grace from the moment of her conception; no part of her heart inhibited God working in and through her. Our fallen hearts, on the other hand, are hindered by our sins and imperfections. This is where Mary, Mother of the Eucharist, can intercede for us, asking God to give us the grace to recognize our need, open our hearts, and receive the power of the Eucharist into those places of brokenness we all have in our hearts. When we receive the Eucharistic heart of Jesus, he brings wholeness into our brokenness, and we are transformed.

To believe is to feel sure that something is true and real. This involves trust and confidence. Mary, in her receiving, believed what had been told her by the angel Gabriel: that she would conceive and bear the Son of

---

3　John Paul II, *Ecclesia de Eucharistia*, 2003, 57.
4　Ibid., 53.
5　Ibid.

God. "Let it be done to me according to your word" (Luke 1:38) was her fiat, her yes to God's will and to his mission. Her conviction of God's love allowed her to give a complete yes even to stepping into the unknown before her. She was confident that God loved her unconditionally, and that wherever she went, whatever she did, whoever she became, this love was the bond that would always attach her to the Creator.

Doubts can often cloud our hearts, creating lies that challenge our identity as beloved of God. At times, the truth of God's love for us seems distant and dry, and we struggle to bring to him our wills, crippled as they are by lack of faith. Mary, Mother of the Eucharist, can intercede for us that we may more fully believe in God's love for us and be set free from all that constrains this truth, so that once again we can walk in the true intimacy of children of God.

At the Visitation Mary greeted her cousin Elizabeth and broke into adoration and praise through the words of the Magnificat: "My soul magnifies the Lord, and my spirit rejoices in God my Savior" (Luke 1:46–47). In her adoration Mary was expressing deep love and reverence for who God is—for his mercy, promises, power, and faithfulness. Her exaltation was an encounter with God.

Like Mary, we were created to praise and glorify God. Eucharistic adoration is a powerful way for us to do this. It brings us into the company of all the angels and saints, strengthens our relationship with God, and brings peace, growth in virtue, and renewal. Adoration connects heaven and earth, strengthening the Body of Christ, and helps us to better love ourselves and others. Mary, Mother of the Eucharist, can intercede for us that we may more fully recognize Jesus' Eucharistic presence and adore him in the Blessed Sacrament, soaring to the heavenly heights and becoming the "praise of his glory" (Ephesians 1:14).

From the Cross, Jesus gave us his mother "whose mission it would be to take us by the hand and lead us to the tabernacle."[6] At each Mass, Mary

---

6 St. Peter Julian Eymard, *Our Lady of the Blessed Sacrament Vol. 7* (Emmanuel Publications), 108.

still stands at the foot of the Cross, beckoning us to receive, believe, and adore the Eucharistic heart of her Son, Jesus. As the priest is preparing the altar, we can ask Mary, Mother of the Eucharist, to help us place in the chalice our own hearts, full as they are of pain, brokenness, sorrows, the needs of others, and the state of the world. Standing spiritually beside Mary, we know in faith that at the moment the bread and wine become the body and blood of Jesus, our brokenness becomes wholeness in his heart. As we step forward to receive the Eucharist and give our own fiat (our "Amen"), we are saying, "Yes, Jesus, I believe this is you."

In receiving his heart of Eucharistic love, we are transformed by the riches he shares with us. As we believe in his promises, we are set free from what keeps us bound, and our hearts expand in gratitude, thanksgiving, and adoration. In faith we believe that the Eucharistic love which we have received can become a wellspring for others. And as we leave Mass, Mary, Mother of the Eucharist, continues to teach us how to receive, believe, and adore and to live the Eucharistic life in our day-to-day walk.

The Sacred Heart of Jesus statue I found that day in the garden shop trash pile now sits enthroned in my family room. Each time I pass it, I smile, remembering how Mary, Mother of the Eucharist, answered my prayer that day: "Mama Mary, bring me into the Heart of Jesus." She has done so by teaching me the wisdom of receiving, believing, and adoring as keys to living a Eucharistic life.

I was inspired to write a prayer about this wisdom. Each time I attend Mass, saying this prayer prepares my heart to enter the heart of Jesus through the heart of Mary, Mother of the Eucharist:

The Eucharistic Heart of Jesus

Receive, Believe, Adore

Within this chalice, I place my heart and all you give to me.
See my brokenness, make me whole, O heart of Jesus.
May I receive and be transformed.
May I believe and be set free.
May I adore and soar to the heavenly heights.
May I receive, believe, and adore.
May my heart be pierced and your love pour forth.
And may this Eucharistic love become a wellspring for others.
May I receive and be transformed.
May I believe and be set free.
May I adore and soar to the heavenly heights.
May I receive, believe, and adore.
Mary, Mother of the Eucharist, pray for us.[7]

Julianne Jackson is a mother, grandmother, Catholic therapist, collector of divine love notes, a writer who speaks, and a consecrated daughter of the St. Francis de Sales Association. She strives "to be who you are and be that well" (St. Francis de Sales) by living Jesus right where the Lord has placed her. To connect and download a copy of the "Receive" prayer, go to *arisecounselingservices.org*.

---

7   Julianne Jackson, "The Eucharistic Heart of Jesus: Receive, Believe, Adore," with ecclesiastical approval.

XVI

MIRROR OF JUSTICE

Mary as the Reflection of Our Eternal Home

Brenda Kostial

For she is the reflection of eternal light, the spotless mirror
of the power of God, the image of his goodness.

—Wisdom 7:26

"Woman, why do you weep?" This question asked of Mary Magdalene at the empty tomb of the Resurrection echoed in my mind, and probably in the minds of my close friends, nearly every Friday evening at our Medjugorje prayer group as I prayed the Litany of Loreto aloud after Adoration and Holy Mass. Every time I got to the invocation "Mirror of Justice," emotion welled up within me, my voice choked, and tears often followed. I had no idea why. I didn't even know what Mirror of Justice meant.

But my heart recognized what my mind couldn't yet grasp: as Mirror of Justice, Our Lady reflects the perfection and glory of God himself in all his truth, goodness, and beauty.[1] And she does so from a place of

---

1   "Mirror of Justice: Sermon by Fr. Tom Lynch. A Day with Mary," posted by A Day with Mary, February 11, 2019, YouTube, https://www.youtube.com/watch?v=8EmRYl3hSNs.

intimate union with our Lord—the same intimate union for which we were all created.

We were created to walk in intimacy with God in the garden. But sin entered the world as Eve engaged with the enemy, entertaining the lie that God couldn't be trusted. In his restorative justice, God willed the Immaculate Conception, a creature who would not succumb to the lies of the evil one, a creature through whom he could send his only-begotten Son into the world to atone for man's sin and restore man's relationship with God. This creature would be the new Eve, the highest honor of her people (see Judith 15:10), the Mirror who would reflect for man both God and himself. Through her devotion and purity of heart, the Mirror of Justice would reflect the fruition of God's original plan for man: to know, to love, and to serve him, and so to come to paradise (see CCC 1721).

It is in this right relationship with God, where we know, love, and serve him, that we are meant to flourish, but for much of my life, I didn't know how to "know" God, only to know about him. I didn't realize that a relationship with him was possible. As a little girl, I prayed to God the Father but thought of him as a distant God whom I would only encounter in heaven. I know now that this is so far from the truth! Our Lady, Mirror of Justice, however, knew and loved God from her conception and lived the Father's plan for her perfectly, and she reflects that to her children, showing us the way.

A mirror must reflect light to create an image. Our Lady reflects the light of Christ, her Son, the eternal glory of God. To reflect with clarity, a mirror must be a clean surface. Our Lady is a spotless mirror, for her soul is pure and her intellect untainted by sin.[2] A mirror reflects the image before it. Our Lady reflects the fullness of the Trinity, for she is daughter of the Most High, spouse of the Holy Spirit, and Mother of Christ. She is the splendor of heaven, bearing the image of God with all of the truth

---

2   Ibid.

and goodness and beauty that is his nature, and because she is a mirror of the divine, she perfectly mirrors his justice.

In his *Summa Theologica*, St. Thomas Aquinas defines justice, one of the four cardinal virtues, as "a habit whereby a man renders to each one his due by a constant and perpetual will."[3] St. John Henry Newman wrote that justice implies all of the virtues at once, "a perfect, virtuous state of soul, righteousness, or moral perfection"—sanctity. Therefore, Our Lady as Mirror of Justice is the mirror of perfect holiness.[4]

Justice is about our responsibilities to God and to others and the way in which we honor and respect the demands of those relationships. We owe God obedience, and to fulfill the moral virtue of religion, which also falls under justice, we are to honor and revere God with worship, devotion, prayer, and sacrifice.[5] It's the first commandment: "You shall love the Lord, your God, with all your heart, with all your soul, and with all your mind" (Matthew 22:37). Oh, but it's so much more than a commandment; it's an invitation to intimacy.

I first got a glimpse of this intimacy when I noticed something in others, something I didn't have that stirred in me a desire for more. They spoke about Jesus differently, knew him differently than I knew him. I recognized an inner joy, an emotional connection with Jesus. My friend's eyes teared up when she spoke about Jesus, and I wondered why I didn't get tears when I talked about him. I knew he was present in the Eucharist and felt joy in receiving him, yet I didn't know how to enter into a relationship with him. As I began to seek him more intentionally, our Lord met me in the depths of my heart, drew me to want to know him more, and taught me to discern his voice.

---

3   Internet Encyclopedia of Philosophy, https://iep.utm.edu/justwest/#SH2b.

4   Fr. Juan Velez, "Mary, Mirror of Justice ~ Cardinal Newman," *John Henry Newman*, May 11, 2014, https://www.cardinaljohnhenrynewman.com/mary-mirror-of-justice-cardinal-newman/.

5   Edward Sri, *The Art of Living* (San Francisco: Ignatius Press, 2021), 206.

In the beauty of God's justice, when we respond to God in obedience and give what he is owed in justice, when we pray and worship and put God in his proper first place in our lives, he responds ever so generously, lavishing us with his love and drawing us into relationship with him. In his goodness, he desires us to know him in the deepest recesses of his Most Sacred Heart. We give him what is owed to him, but we receive so much more.

Completely devoted to God, Our Lady, Mirror of Justice, embodied the joy of fulfilling these virtues, loving him with all her heart, all her soul, and all her intellect. She freely gave her fiat from the purest disposition of heart, recognizing God as Creator and herself as creature, submitting herself entirely to serving him.[6] In Our Lady there was no resistance, only detachment from her own will and a holy resignation to the will of God.

As we follow the model of our mother, she reflects to us what we wouldn't otherwise see: the image of ourselves and what we lack in virtue and holiness.[7] We, too, are called to live a life of holiness, to conform to and follow Christ (see 1 Peter 1:15–16)—to become mirrors of justice like Our Lady. She invites us also to give God the first place in our hearts, to be filled with and reflect his love, to open every part of our hearts and lives to him in total trust. Our intellects are darkened by sin and our hearts impure, but God brings his light and truth as we encounter Jesus in the sacrament of confession, in the Eucharist, and in Sacred Scripture. He illumines our minds and heals our hearts, polishing our souls to better reflect his love.[8] He invites us to detach from the people and things of this world that we hold a little too tightly so as to more intimately attach to him. As our relationship with our Lord deepens, so does our trust.

---

6   Mary of Agreda, *City of God: The Conception*, trans. Fiscar Marison (Alburquerque, NM: Corcoran Publishing Company, 1902), 186.

7   "Mirror of Justice: Sermon by Fr. Tom Lynch. A Day with Mary."

8   "Our Lady Mirror of Justice: Sermon by Fr. Pius Collins o.praem. A Day with Mary," posted by A Day with Mary, April 4, 2024, YouTube, https://www.youtube.com/watch?v=n86uWKf2mdU

And then our Lord allows opportunities for us to emulate Our Lady, to walk in the trust that she reflects. Although he had given me these opportunities before, I discovered this in a more profound way with the death of my mother.

As my sister's words sunk in, repeating the prognosis and short time frame shared by my mom's hospice nurse, my heart fell, and I felt sick to my stomach. This wasn't the way I thought it would happen. I thought my mom would have more time with us. My relationship with my mom had changed in many ways as her Alzheimer's had progressed over the years, but I still had her with me. This last letting go was so final. The last days of my mother's journey to her eternal life had now begun. It was completely out of my control, and I wasn't ready.

But I could also clearly see how our Lord had begun to prepare me. He had done so much inner healing in me over the past several months. He had also prompted me to prepare classroom materials that I wouldn't need for weeks so that all would be ready for a substitute teacher, allowing me to take this time to be with my mom and family.

Our Lord had filled me with incredible peace and an awareness of him walking me through my days. Now, as I sat praying at the side of my mother's bed, waiting and offering my suffering so that God could be glorified in this cross, I thought of Our Lady. Was this what she felt when Jesus was condemned? The journey toward the death of her Son had begun and was completely out of her control. She also probably wanted more time.

Our Lady mirrored the sacrifice of her Son as she watched his condemnation, his scourging, and his suffering on the way to Calvary, where she stood praying at the foot of his Cross, mirroring every virtue that Christ exhibited in perfect submission to the Father's will. She fulfilled all justice in that she would not abandon him but would offer her own suffering as sacrifice in union with his, as she too submitted in complete trust to the will of the Father.[9]

---

9 "The Seven Sorrows of Mary: Powerful Promises & Devotion to Our Lady of Sorrows - Fr. Ripperger," posted by Sensus Fidelium, February 7, 2019, YouTube, https://www.youtube.com/watch?v=tDSsFn-JaXY.

When two people close to me sent me the same message, "surrender," I recognized the Holy Spirit. I needed to trust. I prayed the surrender novena prayer: *O Jesus, I surrender myself entirely to you, take care of everything.*

Instead of clinging to control, I clung in faith to the Rosary of Our Lady and to the Divine Mercy Chaplet of her Son. Our Lady responded with graces, the grace to sing the Hail Mary to my mother, which would come back to me after her passing, and to be at her side with my brother at the precise moment my mom opened one eye and, although unable to speak, fixed her gaze on something before her, her face filled with joy. I turned to my brother, sharing through my emotion the scripture that came to my mind: "No eye has seen, nor ear heard . . . what God has prepared for those who love him" (see 1 Corinthians 2:9)

We don't emulate Our Lady perfectly. She received the body of her Son taken down from the Cross and helped to place him in the tomb. Our Lady's sacrifice fulfilled God's justice. I couldn't bear to be there when the undertaker came for my mother's body. I went instead to Holy Mass where I wept during the consecration, crying out from my heart, "I love you, Mom."

I know the truth of the resurrection and the hope of heaven. *So why do I weep?*

Our Lady surely wept at the death of her Son, yet she mirrored the peace of Christ. She was filled with the Holy Spirit, her trust so great that nothing could disturb her inner peace, not even the crucifixion of her Son, for peace is the place where the presence of our Lord dwells, bearing trials without disturbance.[10]

St. Clare of Assisi once wrote in a letter to St. Francis:

And a peaceful heart comes from finding so much God inside that there is no room for anything else but peace. . . . Ask them to sit and

---

10 "Our Lady Mirror of Justice: Sermon by Fr. Pius Collins o.praem. A Day with Mary."

feel our Lord's presence. Let them know, "There is an inner garden!" Every day we go to the sacred well of peace inside our hearts. As peace becomes more important, our self-importance becomes less. Slowly, we become instruments with a sound that is beautiful and true.[11]

Then we, like Our Lady, Mirror of Justice, begin to reflect the beauty, truth, and goodness of God to those around us, so they too may come to know, love, and serve him, and so to come to paradise (CCC 1721).

For so long I sought God outside of myself, as a distant God, but our Lord is so much nearer than I knew. As St. Clare reminded St. Francis, "God is no further away than our heart."[12] From within this inner garden my heart cries out, "I love you, Lord. May it be done to me according to your word" (Luke 1:38). This is why I weep when I call upon the Mirror of Justice. I long for heaven, and she reflects God, my eternal home.

At the Annunciation, the Archangel Gabriel said to Mary, "Do not be afraid" (Luke 1:30). Do not be afraid to say yes to our Lord, to give him everything as Our Lady did, and then, as she would later tell the servers at the Wedding at Cana, "Do whatever he tells you" (John 2:5).

It's an incredibly beautiful way to live. Let the adventure begin, the journey into the abyss of God's love, and be filled to overflowing, and then mirror that love to the world. Our Lady, the Mirror of Justice, reflects for us the way.

Brenda Kostial writes to invite readers to deeper surrender and intimacy with God, entrusting all to Jesus through our Blessed Mother. A teacher, writer, and speaker, she loves sharing her witness of the peace, joy, wonder, and awe of a life lived for Jesus. Learn more and download a prayer for intimacy at *brendakostial.com*.

---

11 Bruce Davis, "Simple Peace: A Letter to St. Francis of Assisi from St. Clare," *HuffPost*, March 28, 2013. https://www.huffpost.com/entry/simple-peace-a-letter-to-st-francis-of-assisi-from-st-clare_b_2940300.

12 Ibid.

XVII

STAR OF THE SEA

How Mary Steadily Guides Us Through Life's Darkness

Katie Heeney

In the beginning when God created the heavens and the earth,
the earth was a formless void and darkness covered the face
of the deep, while a wind from God swept over the face of the
waters. Then God said, "Let there be light"; and there was light.

—Genesis 1:1–3

After creating the heavens and earth, God gifted us with light. So too, after the conception of our Lord and Savior, came the gift of Mary—a light to help guide us to our Lord when we are lost.

Our Lady, Star of the Sea, shines with this particular beckoning radiance. She is perhaps most well known to seafarers and those who live and work at the world's edge, depicted on canvases, carvings, and jewelry with a signature star of radiant light alongside ships, anchors, and crashing waves. Those who brave rough waters and dangerous nautical voyages ask for her prayers for safe passage, guidance, and hope.

While the title might suggest Mary as Star of the Sea is exclusively an intercessor for those setting sail or living with the ebb and flow of terrestrial tides, she is in fact a guide for us all through the turbulent seas of our everyday lives. We can look to her with expectation, for she will always point us in the direction of salvation.

Without such a guiding light, we can easily lose our way and thus amplify our suffering. I know this sad state very well, as I spent the majority of my life directionless and lost in a vortex of confusion without Christ. I closed my eyes tight, trying to comfort myself through life's typhoons, and struggled against currents to no avail. No solace came from the sources I turned to for guidance. Unlike physical tools for navigation, which we must learn to use and which can become lost, light only requires notice. Thankfully, it can shine through tightly closed eyelids. Mary's gentle starlight awoke in me a desire to open my eyes, and when I did, there was Christ.

The hymn *Ave Maris Stella* invokes Mary as Star of the Sea. The earliest known source of the hymn is found in a collection attributed to Nonker Balbulus, a monk at the Monastery of Saint Gall in Switzerland during the early Middle Ages, but sure attribution is unknown.[1] The hymn hails Our Lady as "bright star of ocean" and asks her to "light on blindness pour" and to "make our way secure."[2] She never fails to deliver on this promise, as we are reminded whenever we pray the Memorare:

> Remember, O most gracious Virgin Mary, that never was it known that anyone who fled to thy protection, implored thy help, or sought thine intercession was left unaided.
>
> Inspired by this confidence, I fly unto thee, O Virgin of virgins, my mother; to thee do I come, before thee I stand, sinful and sorrowful. O Mother of the Word Incarnate, despise not my petitions, but in thy mercy hear and answer me. Amen.

We can trust Our Lady to be an ever-present guiding light when we feel the pull to dive deeply into the fathoms of faith, into the depths of God's divinity, presence, and love. This is where we venture to be

---

1   *Ave Maris Stella,* https://www.encyclopedia.com/religion/encyclopedias-almanacs-transcripts-and-maps/ave-maris-stella

2   Translations of Ave Maris Stella vary, but the meaning expressed in each line remains constant.

formed in Christ and undergo a spiritual metamorphosis that aligns the trajectory of our lives with God's vision. Let us now venture into deeper waters, asking Maris Stella to guide us. Taking a voyage that requires a submersible rather than sails and rigging, we now plunge into the deepest darkness where the Star of the Sea is needed most: into the abyss.

St. Elizabeth of the Trinity was a Carmelite mystic who descended to the depths herself to return with this wise testimony: "'Abyss calls to abyss.' It is there in the very depths that the divine impact takes place, where the abyss of our nothingness encounters the Abyss of mercy, the immensity of the all of God. There we will find the strength to die to ourselves and, losing all vestige of self, we will be changed into love."[3]

St. Elizabeth, inspired by St. John van Ruusbroec and St. John of the Cross's remarks on the topic, further provides us with needed provisions before we attempt our own voyage into the deep, to understand what we are truly being asked to do:

> What is this descent that He demands of us except an entering more deeply into our interior abyss? This act is not "an external separation from external things," but a "solitude of spirit," a detachment from all that is not God. "As long as our will has fancies that are foreign to divine union, whims that are now yes, now no, we are like children; we do not advance with giant steps in love for fire has not yet burnt up all the alloy; the gold is not pure; we are still seeking ourselves; God has not consumed" all our hostility to Him. But when the boiling cauldron has consumed "every imperfect love, every imperfect sorrow, every imperfect fear," "then love is perfect and the golden ring of our alliance is larger than Heaven and earth. This is the secret cellar in which love places his elect," this "love leads us by ways and paths known to him alone; and he leads us with no turning back, for we will not retrace our steps."[4]

---

3 *Saint Elizabeth of the Trinity: Complete Works,* Volume 1 (ICS Publications, 1991. Revised 2023), 130.
4 Ibid., 131.

St. Elizabeth here draws attention to our need for purification, to be refined by a process that involves extreme change—like refining an alloy into pure gold. To be refined ourselves, we will need to undergo a similar transformation, and to do so we must let go of what does not serve us.

St. Elizabeth's enthusiasm for the abyss of God's mercy, as she calls it, as well as the process of transformation, is a testimony to the power of abyssal descent. Let us then be optimistic, for where we are headed is not the darkness of nightmares, or where the enemy dwells, but rather the depths where God's love is so abundant that its immense density creates an enveloping dark. This is the dark of pure trust, where there is no need for us to see. As we sink deeper, we can rely less on the sight of our ocular orbitals and more on our hearts and souls drawn by Mary's light, strongly felt even when out of view, deeper toward God.

As we've heard, to experience God's abyss requires sacrifice, to leave behind what we cannot take with us as we journey ever further into the depths. This is why we need Mary's help as we venture leagues under the waves of our ordinary concerns, routines, and situational sorrows. We need her to help us grow closer to God, because we've become scared of the dark. We are afraid of the unknown, of change, of letting go. To overcome, we need humility, abyssal humility, Mary's humility.

Our resistances are our greatest obstacles. We may dip our timid toes into puddles of faith, but are we willing to jump into the unfathomable depths? To drown to ourselves? To be suffocated by God's abundant density? Those questions are worded deliberately to probe for internal revolt, to test how far we are willing to go for God.

Jesus asks us to give up everything and follow him. Are we willing to leave on shore what does not serve us in that journey, what holds us back from deepening our faith? How attached are we to "external things," to quote St. Elizabeth—to comfort, our routines, and the familiar? What "fancies" do we have that "are foreign to divine union"?[5]

---

5 Ibid.

Like a star, the power of Mary's guiding light comes from its constancy rather than its brightness. Maris Stella twinkled gently, yet unwaveringly, drawing my attention when my faith was barely a drop in a sea, a particle at most, perhaps even just a single molecule. She came to me when my conversion was all but impossible. I was a student of psyche and myth, exploring the world of psychology as taught by Carl Jung, and the process felt enriching. I thought I had found meaning, but in reality, what I found were wonderful stories that delighted me, the way fairy tales captivate a child. When I began to question the ideas of synchronicity and a collective unconscious interconnecting humanity existing without a guiding hand (specifically the guiding hand of God), that was all the invitation the Lord needed. He took that mere atomic particle of doubt and multiplied it to fill an entire ocean within me. How very like our Lord.

The Holy Spirit led me to his spouse in my academic research when it veered into the topic of Polish folklore, seeking to find useful archetypal metaphors in the myths of my Slavic ancestors. Instead, I encountered Mary, and once her light drew my attention, she began to pull me toward her Son. My Catholic faith, dormant since my childhood baptism, became the center of my life—a fact I can still hardly believe. I am truly in awe of how elegantly Mary navigated me to Christ. Today she continues to guide me as I embark on seemingly endless voyages into the unknown. My entire life has become a new unknown, a New World without maps or familiarity of any kind. I find solace in knowing I have Mary as my guide no matter what shape and form my journey takes because she only leads to one salvific destination.

Through her, I came to recognize God's love, both in the moment and looking back. I had an Augustinian realization that God was with me all my life. He never abandoned me. He was everywhere even if I didn't have the eyes yet to see him. He was my inspiration as an artist and the co-creator of all I have made. He knew I would come when he called, through Mary. That I would write this chapter. That I would share with others my deep love for our heavenly mother. How her particular light can lead us all through every manner of darkness, from surface turmoil and enemy allurements, to sinking into God's abyss of divinity.

Mary asked me to take a leap of faith, to leave behind who I thought I was. I was apprehensive initially to shed my whole identity, and I knew it would be painful at times to let go. But Mary asked in a way only a mother can, convincing me, her child, to trust her without question. She helped me to enter into a profoundly fulfilling relationship with Christ, and that is what we receive when we are willing to trade the abyss of our own creation for the abyss of love, of faith, of who we are meant to be with the grace of God.

We began this chapter by recognizing how Mary, Star of the Sea, is a comfort and light that helps us to navigate through the storms of life. We then ventured beneath the waves to understand how her starlight can keep us focused and guide us into a descent of humility to find God in the deepest abyss of his abundance—even when we are afraid to dive in. We discovered how that journey is transformative, precisely because we have to choose to take the plunge. It is then that we learn the only perils we face come when we mistakenly assign high value to what has none at all. Only after we toss overboard the baggage that holds us back from receiving God's love can we become more agile. It is in this process of transformation that we can look to Mary, our north star, and beyond her to whom her light is navigating us: her Son.

Katie Heeney writes from the perspective of an artist, shaped by her experience as a scholar, grounded by her life as a mother and wife, enriched by her Catholic faith. She follows Christ where he leads, often in many unexpected directions. She shares her adventures with readers and viewers looking for camaraderie on parallel journeys into the depths with Mary as a guide at *katieheeney.com*.

XVIII

THE IMMACULATE CONCEPTION

My Mother's Birthday and Lifting the Veil

Heather Lebano

The Immaculate Conception shines like a beacon
of light for humanity in all the ages.

—St. John Paul II

December 8 was my mother's birthday. For me, it was a date filled with cake, candles, laughter, and family. We didn't decorate for Christmas until after her birthday, as if her day marked a threshold into the season of Advent and expectation. Only years later did I discover that December 8 is also the Feast of the Immaculate Conception—a Holy Day of Obligation, set aside by the Church to honor Mary, who was preserved from the stain of sin from the moment of her conception.

While I grew up with faith, attending church and reading Scripture, I was not raised Catholic. I know now that I was always drawn to the Catholic Church. Still, I had a minimal understanding of Mary. All I knew was that she carried Jesus in her womb and delivered him on Christmas. That was the extent of my knowledge of Mary. I had no real sense of her titles, her unique role in salvation history, or her ongoing presence in the life of the Catholic Church.

When I first heard the words "Immaculate Conception," I assumed they meant the miraculous way Jesus was conceived. Like many others, I misunderstood.

It wasn't until my own journey of conversion, which slowly unfolded through my twenties, that I began to realize this feast day wasn't about Jesus' conception at all. It was about Mary's.

This feast is all about the way God, in his mercy, prepared a mother for his Son by preserving her from the stain of original sin. The Immaculate Conception was not just a theological detail; it was the hidden beginning of God's plan of redemption.

Immaculate means "without stain," and the Church teaches that Mary was conceived in the womb of her mother, Saint Anne, without the stain of original sin. But the Immaculate Conception is not just an event; it is a title, a quality, and a virtue of our Blessed Mother, Mary.

When I was fourteen, I moved to an all-girls Catholic high school run by the Sisters, Servants of the Immaculate Heart of Mary (IHMs). It was my first immersion in Catholic life, and it was there that seeds of Marian devotion were planted, though I didn't recognize them for what they were at the time. The sisters' strength, creative hope, fidelity, love, discipline, and deep devotion made a lasting impression on me, even as an outsider.

It was in those years that I first began to hear Mary's name spoken with reverence. Phrases like "Hail Mary, full of grace," "Remember, O most gracious Virgin Mary," and even the mysterious words "*I am the Immaculate Conception*" became familiar. I was intrigued by the Rosary and by the mystery of Mary herself. I would roll the beads between my fingers as I heard the prayers whispered. Though I didn't yet know what they meant, something in me was drawn to them.

The IHM Sisters lived their vocation with joy and love. Even without saying much, their lives were a witness. I hadn't yet realized it, but simply being taught by them was another way Mary was drawing me closer to her and ultimately closer to Jesus. Still, the theology of Mary remained foreign to me. She was a mystery I could not quite grasp. Looking back now, I can see how God was already planting seeds in my heart, waiting for the right time for them to bloom.

It took years before I could begin to understand what the Church actually teaches about the Immaculate Conception. The *Catechism of the Catholic Church* explains:

> The most Blessed Virgin Mary was, from the first moment of her conception, by a singular grace and privilege of almighty God and by virtue of the merits of Jesus Christ, Savior of the human race, preserved immune from all stain of original sin....The splendor of an entirely unique holiness by which Mary is enriched from the first instant of her conception comes wholly from Christ. (CCC 491–492)

Mary was saved by Christ just as we are—but she was saved in a unique way. Grace reached her at the very beginning, so that when Gabriel greeted her with the words "Hail, full of grace, the Lord is with you" (Luke 1:28), it wasn't a poetic phrase. It was a declaration of her identity, the fruit of God's grace at work from her very first moment. She was free from sin, able to offer her whole self without hesitation.

Pope Benedict XVI writes, "Mary's greatness consists in the fact that she wants to magnify God, not herself."[1] That is what the Immaculate Conception makes possible. Her life is not about herself, but about God. Mary is not a detour—she is the vessel God himself chose to bring Jesus into the world. This is why the faithful so often say, "To Jesus through Mary." Her mission is simple: to lead us to him. When we pray the Rosary, we are not idolizing her; we are looking at Jesus through her eyes and allowing her to place our hands in his.

I once heard a priest put it another way: "We make God too small when we see Mary as just any woman. The God who created the stars was in her womb." That truth still stuns me. The God who formed galaxies

---

1 Pope Benedict XVI, *Deus Caritas Est,* December 25, 2005, https://www.vatican.va/content/benedict-xvi/en/encyclicals/documents/hf_ben-xvi_enc_20051225_deus-caritas-est.html.

chose to be formed inside the womb of this holy, humble, undefiled, gentle woman prepared from all eternity to be his mother.

Fr. Francis Fernández writes, "Every aspect of her being shone with the splendour of that harmony with which God had originally wanted to endow all humanity. She was free from all actual sin and from even the slightest moral imperfection . . . through the merits of Christ, Mary received the fullness of grace from Redemption."[2]

Even with all the seeds planted, it wasn't until decades later, on retreat, that I finally felt Mary's presence in a way that moved from my head to my heart. I had been invited to an Advent retreat at the IHM Motherhouse, the same place where my high school graduation Mass was once held.

It was the IHM Sisters who first taught me to begin my day with the Morning Offering: "O Jesus, through the Immaculate Heart of Mary, I offer you my prayers, works, joys, and sufferings of this day. . ." I hardly understood, but I knew that prayer meant something. Later, as my children were taught by the IHMs through their instruction in prayers and catechism, I slowly began to understand more.

At the time of the retreat, our family was enduring difficult circumstances. We were discerning major decisions, praying for clarity, and struggling under the weight of uncertainty.

In the first half of the retreat, the speaker invited us to reflect on our relationship with Jesus. That felt comfortable for me. Jesus was my anchor—my constant friend, loving Father, King, and comforter.

The second half of the retreat was devoted to Mary, and I felt a sense of sadness. I admitted how little connection I had with her, save for my mom sharing her birthday with a solemn feast. Though I had tried to pray the Rosary before, it had never left me feeling "full of grace." I grieved not having grown up with Mary's presence in my life and in my home.

---

2   Francis Fernández-Carvajal, "Immaculate Conception," in *In Conversation With God: Volume 7, Feasts, July–December 7*, 7:353–54 (Hounslow, England: Scepter Publishers, 1993).

I whispered this grief to a friend beside me, admitting, "I don't even know where to begin with her." She smiled gently, touched my arm, and pointed upward. "Look where you're sitting," she whispered. I lifted my eyes. Above me stood a beautiful statue of Our Lady of Grace, arms extended, mantle flowing, gaze tender.

As I sat there in Eucharistic adoration, something within me shifted. It was as though Mary herself lifted a veil, revealing to me the hidden places in my life where she had always been present. She showed me the moments she had quietly guided me, protected me under her mantle, and stood near the foot of my crosses—even before I had words to recognize her. She revealed to me that she had always been guiding my steps toward her Son, teaching me gentleness, leading me to give my fiat while accepting every cross and trusting Jesus' will for my life.

I thought of St. Bernadette at Lourdes, who heard the words, *"I am the Immaculate Conception."* Those words carried power for me, too. Mary was not an abstract doctrine; she was a mother who had been present in my story all along.

That day became a turning point in my life. Staying close to Mary by praying the Rosary daily, I began to notice the graces that flowed from it. I committed myself to not missing again. I left the retreat with clarity and a firm decision on something that changed the trajectory of my family's days ahead.

Mary's presence was not only woven into my story, but also into my mother's. For years, December 8 had been simply her birthday. Though her dad was Catholic, she was not raised in the faith. Her mom had little regard for the faith. But God redeems.

A few years ago, when my father was in the hospital during his final months, something shifted for my mother. She began praying the Rosary. Despite her years of experience as a hospice nurse, with her own health challenges, there was little she could do for my dad in those final months. But she could pray. *And she did.*

I taught her how to pray the Rosary. One day, before heading to the hospital to see my dad, I took my mom to my church where, bead by bead, I taught her the prayer. She turned to me, holding the rosary in her hand, and asked, almost with hesitation: "Would my mom be upset that I am praying the Rosary, praying to Mary?"

I looked at her with tenderness and said, *"You are praying to her Son through Mary. And your mom knows the truth now."*

That moment is etched in my mind. My mom turned toward Mary, who was already holding her, guiding her toward Jesus in her grief. Her question carried the vulnerability of someone opening a new door of faith. My answer was simple but true: devotion to Mary is always devotion to Christ. To Jesus, through Mary.

Over time, my mom would text me daily to say that she prayed the Rosary two or three times a day before and after my dad died. It brought her peace.

The more I reflect, the more I realize how deeply rooted Mary has been in my life and suffering. Both my mom and I came to know her more fully at the foot of the Cross—she, while watching her husband suffer and die; me, while carrying crosses I could not bear on my own, including the long illness and death of my own husband. Mary understands the ache of a widow. She was a widow, too.

Mary teaches us that faith is not lived apart from sorrow. It is lived in the midst of it. Her Immaculate Heart is pierced, yet she remains open, trusting, and faithful. Her "yes" to Gabriel becomes her "yes" at Calvary.

We prayed a Rosary when my husband was in his final hour, and he took his final breath at the moment the words *"Mary's pierced heart,"* were spoken. I have always found that significant.

I have clung to the Rosary, especially in the seasons of loss and widowhood, turning my own tears into a deeper faith because of her example. I have prayed for a heart like hers: gentle, obedient, docile, and willing to say yes even when I do not understand.

Our Lady was present during my moments of suffering and sorrow, when I was being asked to carry crosses that forced me to the foot of the Cross, exactly where Mary found herself with her Son.

Looking back now, I see how December 8—the Feast of the Immaculate Conception *and* my mother's birthday—was always quietly pointing me toward Mary, Jesus' mother, just as Jesus pointed his followers to her in his final moments: *"Here is your mother" (John 19:27).*

She is the one I very much need, the one who has tucked me under her mantle long before I recognized her presence. She is the one who brought me to her Son and to the Catholic Church as she guided my steps along the path to my conversion just before I married at twenty-seven. She is the one who steadies me to say yes, even in suffering, and the one who still whispers at the foot of the Cross: "Trust him. Say yes."

As you reflect on the Immaculate Conception, I encourage you to ask the Blessed Virgin Mary to pull back the veil in your own life. She has been with you, too—guiding your steps toward her Son, wrapping you in her mantle of grace. Her Immaculate Heart will never stop leading you home—and home is always to her Son.

Heather Lebano is a Catholic writer and creator of House of Love and Laughter, a space where faith, family, and creativity meet. A widow and mother of four, she writes from the heart about grief, healing, and hope—about learning to cling to Christ and to notice grace in the ordinary. Guided by Our Lady and the communion of saints, her work offers a soft place to land for weary souls searching for light. Learn more at *houseofloveandlaughter.com.*

XIX

Our Lady of Sorrows

Revealing the Power and Purpose of Suffering

Elizabeth Leon

And a sword will pierce your own soul too.

—Luke 2:35

Our Lady of Sorrows found me when I needed her the most. In September 2017, my husband and I traveled to Italy on a vacation-turned-pilgrimage after receiving a life-limiting diagnosis for our son, John Paul Raphael, still safely tucked in my womb. Every altar, every Mass, every saint was an opportunity to lay my broken heart before the Lord. We prayed at the tomb of St. Paul the Apostle, St. John Paul the Great, St. Francis of Assisi—so many warriors to intercede for one tiny baby and his terrified mother.

The day before our return, we spent a whirlwind twenty-four hours in Florence. After touring the main sights, we strolled through a quiet square on the way to lunch and decided to explore a lovely church tucked under a colonnade. As my eyes adjusted to the cool, dim interior, a statue in front of the altar grabbed my attention. Our Lady stood draped in black, her eyes downcast, with seven iron swords piercing her heart. Her vulnerable display of suffering stunned me, and I gazed in reverent awe.

Before I could approach her, the bells rang. We were surprised to have arrived just in time for holy Mass, and I soon discovered it was the Feast of Our Lady of Sorrows, September 15. Tears sprang to my eyes. It was no coincidence to have discovered this church on this day at this time.

Our pilgrimage began nine days prior at the Basilica of St. Peter in Rome. I wept at the feet of the *Pietà*, pierced by the agony of Our Lady cradling her crucified son and by the brutal truth that my child, too, would die. I wanted to press my face into the marble folds of her veil. Mary stood for so long at the foot of the Cross and now, cradling Jesus, she sinks to the rock of Golgotha. Crushed beneath my own suffering, I drew consolation from the truth that Mary is a mother who knows the weight of sorrow.

She knew my heart was being pierced. She knew I was terrified of my son's death. She knew that a tsunami of grief would tear through my life and nothing would ever be the same again. She gave me permission to feel everything a mother feels when watching her son die, along with the hope that suffering would not be the end of my story.

The first mention of Our Lady's sorrow is in the Gospel of Luke when the prophet Simeon declares to Mary that a sword will pierce her heart (Luke 2:35). Devotion to Our Lady of Sorrows followed the publication of the *Stabat Mater*, attributed to Jacopone da Todi, and the founding of the Servite order, an order dedicated to Mary under the title of Mother of Sorrows. A feast specific to Our Lady of Sorrows was first placed on the Roman calendar in 1727, and in 1913, Pope St. Pius X permanently established the memorial on September 15, the day after the Exaltation of the Holy Cross.[1] Our Lady of Sorrows also appeared to St. Brigid of Sweden (1303–1373), revealing many graces that could come through devotion to her sorrowful heart.

The traditional seven sorrows of Mary developed over time and are rooted in scripture. They were approved by Pope Pius VII in 1815: the

---

1   Enzo Lodi, *Saints of the Roman Calendar: Including Feasts Proper to the English-Speaking World* (Staten Island, NY: Alba House, 1992), 264.

prophecy of Simeon, the flight to Egypt, the loss of the Child Jesus in the Temple, meeting Jesus on the way of the Cross, the crucifixion of Jesus, Jesus being taken down from the Cross, and Jesus being laid in the tomb (John 19:39–42).

I have known deep suffering, not just the death of my child, but the heartbreak of divorce, the betrayal of adultery, and the violation of abuse. Our Lady of Sorrows understands the landscape of my heart. If she were only Our Lady of Victory or Queen of Peace, I might not be comfortable turning to her with my suffering, but our *Mater Dolorosa* has swords piercing her heart. She lived through the darkest days of humanity and is not afraid to walk with us in ours. She stands with us and for us at the foot of the Cross, a silent witness to our suffering and grief. She sits with us when we can no longer stand, a compassionate presence in our aching disappointments.

Mary is every mother who has ever lost a child or wept at the world's cruelty to her children. She is every woman who knows hardship, exile, poverty, or the loss of a spouse. She knows what it is to be anxious, afraid, and powerless. Mary longs to help us carry our crosses. She loves us with a mother's heart and invites us to let her soothe our deepest wounds. She models an authentic example of vulnerability and trust through her surrender to the life the Father had planned for her—one that likely looked very different than the one she imagined for herself.

Our Lady of Sorrows gave me courage to embrace the mission the Lord had for my life. I wanted to stay at the *Pietà* in Rome, crumpled and weeping on the floor, but the woman I saw standing in the aisle of that Florentine church was not crushed by grief. She was steadfast in the face of suffering. Her swords weren't tucked beneath her mantle but unflinchingly revealed. Her face was not devoid of pain but transformed by it. Mary is often depicted as stepping on the head of a serpent, for her heel has crushed the lies that our suffering is punishment or rebuke. She waits with us in our humanity and then beckons us to take up our cross and follow her to Jesus.

Jesus could have given us his mother at any point, but he chose to do so during the hours of both his and Mary's greatest suffering (see John 19:26–27). She is our mother of seven sorrows. And why seven? Were there not in fact seven hundred sorrows (and more) in Mary's life? The reason is symbolic. Biblically, the number seven expresses completion and fulfillment. There are seven days of Creation in Genesis, seven spirits before the throne in Revelation, seven sacraments, seven gifts of the Spirit. Jesus tells Peter to forgive not just seven times, but seventy-seven times, expressing infinite perfection. To suffer completely, to suffer well, and to receive the fullness of what the Lord wants to offer us spiritually in and through our sufferings, we must suffer with Our Lady of Sorrows.

What can we learn from Mary's example, mourning and weeping in this valley of tears?

Our Lady of Sorrows teaches us that suffering is personal, suffering is meaningful, and suffering is powerful. Mary was a woman convinced of her identity. Her life was not the absence or denial of suffering, but the integration of it. She doesn't show us the swords in her heart to draw attention to her pain, but to remind us of its power.

Suffering is personal. Mary's suffering was no accident. She was prepared by God before she was born to be the mother of our Lord. God knew the swords that would pierce her heart. While certainly God chose Mary for special graces, we too are beloved of God and held within his perfect and permissive will. Each cross He allows is perfectly designed for us. It is not a sign that we are rejected or unworthy but rather a personal invitation to unite our sufferings to Jesus.

When my son died, I fled to the foot of the Cross. I cried out to the Lord, "Why me, why this, why now?" and longed to hear him answer my lament. In response, he gave me his mother. Mary helped me grow in surrender and trust. In the darkness of grief, my heart cracked open so completely that I could finally let the Lord love me in the deepest recesses of my wounds. Mary helped me claim my true identity and become more of the woman I was meant to be, not despite my suffering, but through it.

Mary's sufferings also teach us that suffering is meaningful. Paragraph 1505 of the *Catechism of the Catholic Church* states: "By his passion and death on the cross Christ has given a new meaning to suffering: it can henceforth configure us to him and unite us with his redemptive Passion." The Lord prepared Mary to be configured to Christ through her Immaculate Conception. She did not need suffering to purify her heart, but she accepted suffering as the mother of the Suffering Servant. In our lives, suffering is a pathway to holiness.

Years before John Paul Raphael died, I wrestled with the crushing weight of unworthiness and rejection after my first husband's adultery and our bitter divorce. For months, I lay flattened beneath the wreckage of our broken marriage, hemmed in by accusations, lies, and grief. As I struggled to heal, a dear friend consoled me with these life-changing words: *"I know you are wounded and bleeding, but every scar that you have makes you look more like Jesus."* As I drew closer to the Lord and Our Lady of Sorrows, grace flooded my broken heart. It is a divine paradox that the furrows of my darkest moments birthed a garden of faith and hope that, in time, brought me great peace and purpose.

Finally, I have learned from Mary that suffering is powerful. Our Lady of Sorrows reminds us that our suffering is not the end of the story; resurrection is. Christ's suffering and death were powerful: the forgiveness of sin and the redemption of humanity. In the perfection of her Immaculate Heart, Mary bore more suffering than any other human. In humility and surrender, she followed God's will and became the mediatrix of all grace.[2]

Through Christ, our suffering also has power. The *Catechism* states: "Suffering, a consequence of original sin, acquires a new meaning; it becomes a participation in the saving work of Jesus" (1521). The greater the love, the greater the suffering. Mary suffered more than any other human ever has or will because of her love. But she also offers the hope,

---

2   Pope Leo XIII, *Iucunda Semper Expectatione*, September 8, 1894, §11.

dare I say the promise, that our great suffering can become great love: love for her, love for our Lord, and love for others. Our suffering is not for nothing. The power of the resurrection is waiting to be activated in our broken hearts through surrender to God's will. The Lord never allows a cross that can't be glorified, but we have to do our part.

During my divorce, I struggled to surrender like a thrashing toddler who didn't get her way. Surrender felt like death, and it was a death of sorts—the death of what I thought was best for my life. The Lord was kind and faithful in loving me through my weakness and doubt. When I received my son's life-limiting diagnosis six years later, I remembered where to go. I drove straight to the adoration chapel at our parish and fell to my knees beneath the monstrance. This was my Calvary—one arm wrapped around the foot of the Cross and the other reaching for Mary's hand. Trusting Jesus and leaning on Mary would be the only way through this valley of tears. My surrender allowed the Lord to use my suffering for his purpose and gave me courage to see my suffering as part of the love story the Lord was writing in my life. When we join Mary at the foot of the Cross, our "wounds can become portals of grace for ourselves and others."[3] In time, and with grace, my suffering birthed a mission of hope and healing.

In his book *The Glories of Mary*, St. Alphonsus Liguori speaks as Jesus: "My wounds are ever-flowing fountains of grace; but their streams will reach no one but by the channel of Mary."[4] What are the seven sorrows in your life? You may never know the death of a child, and I pray you don't, but you will know sorrow. You do know grief. Mary stands with her swords vulnerably on display, reminding us that our suffering has power and purpose. She is waiting as a channel of grace in this valley of tears, faithfully leading us to Jesus.

---

3   Kelly Breaux, founder of Red Bird Ministries, personal communication.

4   St. Alphonsus Liguori, *The Glories of Mary* (New York: Benziger Brothers, 1902), 88.

Elizabeth Leon is a Catholic speaker and writer and the founder of the *Journey of the Beloved*, a ministry that inspires and equips others to find freedom and healing in Christ. She is the award-winning author of *Let Yourself Be Loved: Big Lessons from a Little Life* and also serves as the Director of Family Support for Red Bird Ministries. Find Elizabeth online at *elizabethleon.org*.

XX

MADONNA OF THE GRAPES

Loving Our Priests with a Heart Like Mary's

Shauna Occhipinti

Do whatever he tells you.

—John 2:5

Hanging in my foyer, in a vintage gold frame, is an image of Our Lady holding the Christ Child on her lap. In her right hand sits a cluster of grapes that she gazes down upon as she offers them to her Son. His hand rests on the grapes, ready to pluck one. He demurely peeks out from underneath his mother's mantle.

This image was given to me by my own mother about ten years ago when she and my dad were downsizing. As one with an eye always fixed on her eternal home, my mom used this move as the catalyst to begin gifting a few of her "treasures" to those she loved. She asked me and my eight brothers and sisters to walk around our family home and choose a few.

I refused.

While I supported my parents in moving to a home that would better suit their needs in this new season, I was uncomfortable "picking through" their things. In her motherly wisdom, my mom knew I would one day regret this, so she chose for me. Her handwriting of my name on the back of this unique Marian image now marks it as mine.

For many years, this image simply spoke to me of home and motherhood. It connected me to my mom and reminded me of her years of cultivating a faith- and family-centered home. I grew to appreciate this artwork even more on the day I learned its name and how it also connected me to my heavenly mother, and to her priestly sons.

In the 1640s, Pierre Mignard painted *La Vierge à la grappe*—the Virgin of the Grapes (also known as Madonna of the Grapes). It was just one of his numerous Madonna and Child panels, but apparently one of his most popular. At a time when European artists were flocking to Italy to marvel at and learn from Michelangelo's masterpieces, French artist Mignard was drawn to the art of Raphael. It is said that he modeled many of his Virgin and Christ Child pieces after Raphael's Madonnas.

This Virgin of the Grapes was reportedly commissioned for King Louis XIV's private chapel at Versailles. This image, created for private devotion, now hangs for the world to see at the Louvre in Paris, France. It is a painting as deep in Catholic symbolism as it is beautiful.

The grapes foreshadow the Blood of Jesus, which he would shed for us all. They may also point us to Jesus' first miracle at the Wedding of Cana, a miracle granted at the urging of his mother. This first miracle of turning water into wine, at the start of Jesus' public ministry, would soon lead to the gift of his body and blood and a sword of sorrow piercing his mother's heart. On the table is a bowl of apples that hearken back to mankind's fall, which Jesus' death and resurrection would redeem.

Our Lady gently holds her Son. She offers him the grapes, this symbol of his sacrifice, and yet gazes down upon them with a surrendered smile. Her fiat is evidenced even here. The pair is lit with a soft light, illuminated with grace, while the scene surrounding them is dark.

This image reminds me how Our Lady often prepares the ground in our lives for her Son. Like a good mother, she sets the table for a feast of her Son's love and offers a gentle but clear invitation to us to follow him. As she did with Jesus at Cana, she often gently prompts us to step into our own calling. Long before I understood this image's symbolism, knew its name, or how this particular Marian art would weave through my own life, I loved it. Beauty is like that, isn't it? It draws us to what is true and good.

Two years ago, when our pastor was sick and the weight of our large parish fell on the shoulders of our much younger pastoral associates, I felt called to begin praying more faithfully for our priests. This time came on the heels of the Covid years, as more reports of priestly abuse were making headlines, and as I was struggling with frustration about how some of our priestly shepherds handled these challenges. I frankly felt we had been abandoned by those anointed to minister to us. I was given more to complaining about our priests than to praying for them. But I slowly sensed the need to turn my sorrowful gripes into loving prayers.

I began in small ways. As a SoulCore Rosary leader at my parish, I included our priests in our weekly rosary intentions. A few books were then added to my reading list that stressed the importance of praying for our priests. And then, just a year ago, I was asked to participate in a new ministry at our parish—a quiet, veiled ministry for priestly prayers called the Seven Sisters Apostolate.

The mission of the Seven Sisters Apostolate is to find seven women in a parish to agree to pray for a particular priest for one hour in adoration on a specific day each week. The invitation to participate in this apostolate beckoned my heart. As I perused their website to learn more, I scrolled down to their patron saints, and my breath caught in my chest.

There sat the image of the Madonna of the Grapes—the same image hanging in my foyer.

The Seven Sisters' website explains why the Madonna of the Grapes serves as one of the ministry's three patron saints. "This image and title of Our Lady is indicative of how intimately she holds not only Jesus, but those chosen in persona Christi—his priests—close to her heart, ever encouraging the centrality of the Eucharistic life."[1]

My first thought was, "There is no altar and no typical depiction of the Eucharist. Why was this image chosen for a Eucharistic mission?" But as art often does, the symbolism allows the true meaning depicted to shine brighter. As Flannery O'Connor once wrote, "The truer the symbol, the deeper it leads you, the more meaning it opens up."[2] As I read further and contemplated deeper, I understood.

Dr. Elizabeth Lev, an art historian, explains this image's connection to the Eucharistic sacrifice made present today through the anointed hands of our Catholic priests: "Our Lady holds Jesus securely, she does so tenderly and lightly, for he belongs not to her alone but to the whole world. Jesus glances from beneath the security of her veil; how close is Mary to His veiled Eucharistic presence!"[3]

Dr. Lev continues by drawing attention to how softly Mary holds Jesus' body, her hand resting on the white tunic he wears. "The cloth recalls the humeral veil, through which the priest holds the consecrated host, the Body of Christ. Her contact with his actual flesh on the other hand, emphasizes the humanity and vulnerability of Christ."

It was Jesus, the great High Priest, who instituted the ministerial priesthood. Our priests serve "by virtue of the sacrament of Holy Orders" (CCC 1548) in the person of Christ. It is through their ministerial priesthood that we are fed at the Eucharistic table. It is through their service that we are reconciled with Christ in the Sacrament of Reconciliation. It is through them that the outward signs of the sacraments bring God's inward grace to our lives.

---

1 "Madonna of the Grapes," www.sevensistersapostolate.org/patron-saints/.

2 Flannery O'Connor, "The Nature and Aim of Fiction" in *Mystery and Manners: Occasional Prose*, selected and edited by Sally and Robert Fitzgerald (Farrar, Straus & Cudahy, 1969).

3 Dr. Elizabeth Lev, "Pierre Mignard, La Vierge à la grappe," www.sevensistersapostolate.org/patron-saints/.

At their ordination, our priests' souls are forever changed. They are marked with an "indelible spiritual character" (CCC 1582) that sets them apart as a "representative of Christ, Head of the Church, in his triple office of priest, prophet, and king" (CCC 1581). And precisely because they are set apart by Christ for his Church, our priests are prime targets of the devil. They need our help in their daily spiritual combat against the powers of darkness.

St. John Vianney, patron of the priesthood, and one of the other patrons of the Seven Sisters, knew this most intimately through his own life and ministry. He understood that when Satan wants to destroy the Church, he often targets her priests. "When people want to destroy religion, they begin by attacking the priest; for when there is no priest, there is no sacrifice: and when there is no sacrifice, there is no religion."[4]

Although I have fortunately had close relationships with priests throughout my life, thanks in large part to my dad's diaconate vocation, I never before faithfully prayed for them. But all Catholics are called to do so. It is part of our sharing in the Christian role we were anointed for at our baptism. "The Christian faithful, for their part, should realize their obligations to their priests," St. Paul VI encourages us. All the faithful are called to "help their priests by prayer and work insofar as possible so that their priests might more readily overcome difficulties and be able to fulfill their duties more fruitfully."[5]

Christ himself even instructs us to pray for our priests: "The harvest is plentiful, but the laborers are few; therefore ask the Lord of the harvest to send out laborers into his harvest" (Luke 10:2). We can each bear fruit in the life of the Church through our prayers for the Lord's laborers, his priests.

---

4   St. John Vianney, quoted in Kathleen Beckman, L.H.S., *Praying for Priests: An Urgent Call for the Salvation of Souls* (Sophia Institute Press, 2014), 3.

5   Pope Paul VI, *Presbyterorum Ordinis*, December 7, 1965, no. 9, *www.vatican.va/archive/hist_councils/ii_vatican_council/documents/vat-ii_decree_19651207_presbyterorum-ordinis_en.html.*

Mary, as the mother of the eternal High Priest, has a special love for her priests. She "sees in the priest a greater resemblance to the image of her son than in any other Christian of equal holiness."[6] Now, whenever I walk into my foyer and gaze up at the Madonna of the Grapes, it speaks more deeply to me of our priests' plight and our responsibility to support them and share in their ministry through our prayers. It reminds me to implore Mary's intercession for all of our priests—those I'm blessed to know and those I will never meet.

"Do whatever he tells you," Mary directed the servants at the Wedding at Cana (John 2:5). In this image of the Madonna of the Grapes, she seems to say the same to us. It is the invitation of a gentle and loving mother who knows just what we need and when we need it. It is the directive of a celebration that will lead to a sorrowful Calvary that will open the door to eternal life. It is the call for all invited into her Son's ministerial priesthood. It is the invitation to each of us today who share in her Son's priesthood through our baptism. And so I try to answer that call through my daily prayers. Will you?

Mother Mary, Madonna of the Grapes, Mother of all priests, you tenderly held in your hands the eternal High Priest. You prepared him for his sacrifice through your daily acts of motherly love. Look upon all our priests today and wrap them under your motherly mantle. For the priest who washed us in baptismal waters, bringing us to new life in your Son: pray for him. For the priest who first reconciled us to your Son through the Sacrament of Reconciliation: pray for him. For the priest who first fed us with the Body and Blood of your Son: pray for him. For the priest who witnessed our marriage vows: pray for him. For the priest who regularly feeds us at the Eucharistic table of your Son: pray for him. For the priest who today is feeling alone and abandoned: pray for him. For the priest facing temptation: pray for him. For the faithful and stalwart priest: pray for him. You who knew the mystery

---

6   Beckman, *Praying for Priests*, #29.

of joy and sorrow most intimately through your fiat, give our priests bold courage to say yes each day as they live out their vocation. Enliven in all of our priests a deep love for your Son in the Eucharist and draw their hearts ever closer to your motherly heart. Amen.

Shauna Occhipinti writes to bear witness to God's grace. She lives in Georgia with her husband and twin sons. She is passionate about holistic health, helping women joyfully embrace their feminine design and find healing at the hem of the Divine Physician. As a SoulCore leader, she welcomes others under Mary's mantle through the contemplative prayers of the Rosary and functional movement. See *shaunaocchipinti.com*.

XXI

MARY OF THE VISITATION

My Mission from the Walking Madonna

Laurie Ann Pandorf

*During those days Mary set out and traveled to
the hill country in haste to a town of Judah.*

—Luke 1:39

For as far back as I can remember, I have always been fascinated with the Visitation. As a child, I would lie on the floor in my living room, open up our family Bible, turn to the colorful pages on the mysteries of the Rosary, and stop at the one where Mary and her cousin Elizabeth embrace on the doorstep of Elizabeth's home, marveling at the sacred secret of their hidden blessings.

As the youngest in my family, born on the later end of the boomer generation, I was the baby of the family for quite a while. With no new pending births in sight, I was thrilled when I learned my best friend's mother was pregnant with her third child.

Tricia was born when I was eight years old. I remember holding her as an infant, as she was my first, worried about her weak neck and cautious about the soft spot on her head. Whenever I got the chance, I would sneak into the nursery to catch a glimpse of her, sleeping peacefully in the wooden cradle near the door, unaware that my connection to her was awakening my own maternal instincts.

There is so much mystery surrounding pregnancy and childbirth. It's a moment every mother remembers and can recall in vivid detail. This was especially true for Mary, the first disciple, who conceived Jesus under the most extraordinary circumstances. Captured in the Gospel of Luke, it is the only narrative focused on Mary's willing and unconditional participation in salvation history and her sharing of the Good News. Although I am just one person saved by her Son, the events of the Visitation remain significant in Church history and in my own spiritual journey.

The feast day was officially established by Pope Urban VI in 1389, but it had been adopted by the Franciscan Order and named the Visitation of Mary before 1263 and quickly spread to the faithful.[1] Prior to that, the Gospel account from Luke was read on July 2 in the Byzantine Empire on the feast of the "Deposition in the Basilica of the Holy Garment of the Theotokos."[2] The garment was Mary's sash, venerated as a relic, which was moved to its place of honor in Constantinople.

The purpose of establishing the feast was to bring peace and unity to a divided Church and to end the Great Western Schism, a split in the Roman Catholic Church due to political differences. Pope Urban implored the Blessed Mother's intercession, hoping that the beauty and joy surrounding the miraculous events of the Visitation would soften hearts and prompt rival sects to reconcile and reunite. The Schism was not healed immediately; it took a few years for the division to end and

1   "Feast of the Visitation of the Blessed Virgin Mary," Vatican News, May 7, 2022, https://www.vaticannews.va/en/liturgical-holidays/feast-of-the-visitation-of-the-blessed-virgin-mary.html.

2   Katie Richards, "Feast of the Visitation of the Blessed Virgin | National Shrine of Mary, Mother of the Church," National Shrine of Mary, Mother of the Church | Honoring Mary and All Mothers. May 31, 2024. https://thenationalshrineofmarymotherofthechurch.com/feast-of-the-visitation-of-the-blessed-virgin-mary/.

for Rome to show itself once again to be the "one, holy, Catholic and apostolic Church" (CCC 811).

The feast of the Visitation was changed to May 31 in 1969, after the Second Vatican Council, to better align with the liturgical calendar, placing it between the Annunciation (March 25) and the birth of John the Baptist (June 24). That was the same year and month I received my First Holy Communion and, as one of the communicants, led the traditional May Crowning, a glorious Catholic ritual honoring our Queen Mother.

For most of my life, Mary was as still as that statue in my parish church, frozen in time, staring serenely upon those seeking help. Although I know she freely and actively gave her fiat at the Annunciation, it still seemed to me that life was happening *to* Mary, while she remained obedient, quietly accepting her responsibility. However, that understanding began to shift a few years ago when I completed a 54-Day Rosary Novena, a devotion that consists of reciting the Rosary every day for fifty-four days—twenty-seven days in petition of a request, followed by another twenty-seven days in thanksgiving (whether the request has already been granted or not).

Upon completing the novena, I drove to our local Marian shrine in a nearby town to attend Mass. As often happens with prayer, God's answers do not always match our requests. So, although I was praying for emotional and mental healing for my adult son, Mary interceded with a different response and assignment for me. She unveiled three signs in this order: the phrase *Abundant Life*, a Lauren Daigle song entitled "Rescue," and a bumper sticker that read, "It's a child, not a choice."

The virtues that Mary exemplified for the whole Church through the Visitation, and what she shared with me personally after that novena, have profoundly impacted my spiritual journey. She is not only a witness of abiding faith and deep humility, but a woman with a *mission* to become the Mother of God and our spiritual mother in service of all God's children.

Mission, although a familiar concept, was something I was just beginning to sense unfolding in my life. Years prior to completing that novena, I had begun praying for pregnant moms and their babies. This was prompted by witnessing a close friend lose her baby in the womb during the second trimester at twenty-six weeks, and a colleague lose two granddaughters, stillborn at full term. I attended the wake for one of those babies, and I will never forget the image of that tiny casket. Both devastating losses led me to write a poem about those sweet babies, tender buds replanted in the rose garden of heaven, closer to the heart of the Father, given as a keepsake of remembrance for grieving mothers.

After receiving my three messages from Mary, I knew God wanted more from me. Specifically, he wanted me to support struggling pregnant mothers. As a teacher, I thought I could best serve through a literacy initiative. In my quest to provide support by teaching young mothers, or in organizing a book drive for their babies, I found myself on the Sisters of Life website signing up to become a Coworker of Life.

This role requires both spiritual and pastoral support through prayer and providing for logistical needs, such as driving moms to appointments or food shopping, or helping with household chores. Because I live sixty miles away from the Sisters' Visitation Convent in New York City, the likelihood that there might be a woman in my area to assist was low. But God and Mary knew I was right where they needed me to be, and assigned me to a young mother eight miles away. With a grateful heart, I had the privilege of accompanying her through the birth of her son, and in the celebration of his second birthday.

As the concept of mission was continuing to emerge in me, I joined a Blessed is She virtual event to learn more. After taking copious notes, I followed up with a visit to my local adoration chapel for more guidance. To discover our mission, we were encouraged to write a letter to Jesus, asking him to show us who we need to help. During my meditation, I felt Jesus say that I was stepping into a bigger anointing, where my witness, prayers, and actions would be needed. Then he showed me Mary, his Holy Mother, sitting with me first, then comfortably moving up and down the pews acknowledging everyone there.

When I returned home, I searched what I had been shown and discovered the *Walking Madonna*, a bronze statue on the lawn of a cathedral in Salisbury, England.[3] The statue was designed and erected in order to convey the truth that Mary is indeed a woman in motion—not an image from the past, frozen in time, but a vibrant, active spiritual mother for all times.

This brought to mind the Gospel of Luke, when Mary immediately begins her mission by setting out in haste to visit Elizabeth, who lived in the hill country of Judah (Luke 1:39). This was roughly an eighty-mile trip, which would have taken three to four days on foot.[4] For Mary, newly pregnant and bursting with emotion, I like to think those traveling days were an opportunity to reflect on and pray about the magnitude of the call on her life, not to mention all the questions she might have had for her dear cousin, who had struggled for years with infertility. I also appreciate that "Mary remained with her about three months" (Luke 1:56), not only to support Elizabeth, but to prepare herself to give birth to Jesus, alone and away from home.

According to theologian Dr. Edward Sri, this movement is also meant to be understood as a spiritual journey. The Revised Standard Version of the Bible (Catholic edition) uses the words *arose and went.* From the original Greek, Dr. Sri explains that the translation describes "the beginning of a new action," and "to go or to walk." Additionally, when used in other parts of Luke's gospel, those words also imply "great spiritual effort and a journey with a divine purpose."[5]

The *Walking Madonna* travels alongside all of us sinners. And she has shown me my own mission, which encompasses mothers facing fertility challenges, pregnancy, labor and birth, as well as baptisms, godparents,

---

3 "Exploring Walking Madonna by Elisabeth Frink," *Singulart Magazine*, May 20, 2024, https://www.singulart.com/blog/en/2024/05/20/walking-madonna-by-elisabeth-frink/.

4 Edward P. Sri, *Walking with Mary: A Biblical Journey from Nazareth to the Cross* (New York: Image, 2017), 66.

5 Ibid., 66–67.

grandparents, and women who miscarry or who deliver stillborn babies. I also have a particular heartache and personal prayer for mothers who suffer from the shame of abortion, as that is a heavy burden to bear even with the mercy of God's forgiveness and the reassurance of our Holy Mother's steadfast love.

The Walking Madonna perseveres as a spiritual mother for all and serves as a powerful role model as each of us considers our unique mission and purpose as active disciples of her Son.

My connection to Mary of the Visitation has spanned across my entire life. When I consecrated myself to Jesus through Mary, I chose the Feast of the Visitation as my consecration day. When I have the opportunity to recite the Rosary in a community, and it's a Monday or a Saturday when we pray the Joyful Mysteries, I always ask to lead the second decade. And when we begin our closing prayers at my weekly Fellowship Prayer Group, I recite the Fatima prayer and conclude with, "Mary, Mother of Life, pray for us," in honor of Mary of the Visitation.

When I returned to my faith after a twenty-five year absence, I started a blog to practice my skills as a writing teacher and reflect upon my renewed faith. One day, after storms devastated the midwest, a newspaper photographer captured an image of a statue of the Blessed Mother holding baby Jesus. Sprawled on the ground below were branches and uprooted trees, yet Mary and Jesus were unscathed, surrounded by four strong limbs, pillars resting on each corner of the base of the statue. I wrote a post about that image, which I entitled "Majestic Warriors,"[6] and wrote this poem as a reminder of the dignity of life and to embrace my mission as protector and spiritual mother, helping to heal fellow sisters, with our Walking Madonna leading the way:

---

6   Laurie Pandorf, "Majestic Warriors #SOL17," *The Author's Purpose*, March 18, 2017, https://theauthorspurpose.com/2017/03/18/majestic-warriors-sol17.

The Protectors

Awakening to stillness
one winter's morn,
dusk escaping—daylight mourns . . .
Majestic limbs loom in the light
erect and tall, braving the night.
Harrowing sorrows, sin and strife,
battling and protecting innocent life.

Laurie Ann Pandorf is continually amazed in discovering the hidden gems of our Catholic faith. After her reversion twelve years ago, she is an active lector, prayer group leader, retreat team mentor, and contributing author to *Cloud of Witnesses*. She will soon launch *thewellofgrace.com*, where she hopes to share her spiritual journey and mission from the Walking Madonna with fellow sojourners. Meanwhile, you can reach her at *pandorf7@comcast.net*.

XXII

THE VIRGIN OF THE REVELATION

How Mary Always Leads Us to the Word Made Flesh

Sharon Perkins

*God graciously arranged that the things he had once revealed
for the salvation of all peoples should remain in their entirety,
throughout the ages, and be transmitted to all generations.*

—Dei Verbum, 7

One December morning in Mrs. Orchard's third grade class, we were asked to bring a Bible to school so that we could all read the Christmas story together. We dutifully brought our Bibles—me lugging my family's massive, red, leatherbound coffee table Catholic Bible replete with full-color portraits of popes and cardinals, and everyone else carrying their personal copies of the King James Version. My teacher was fascinated and bemused; my eight-year-old self was shocked and a little embarrassed.

As a cradle Catholic growing up in the Bible Belt in the 1960s, I wasn't well acquainted with reading the Scriptures. Sure, I knew the stories backwards and forwards from my children's Bible, and I was exposed to the readings during Mass, but I had never really read the text for myself. I certainly couldn't quote chapter and verse like my Southern Baptist friends! And I had even heard and read the claim that the Catholic religion wasn't really "biblical" because we followed beliefs and practices that weren't mentioned explicitly in the Bible. Since I couldn't readily refute those claims, I began to have my doubts about Catholicism.

These doubts followed me all the way to college—a Catholic university, no less! (Wouldn't you know that it was the only one that awarded me a substantial scholarship?) It was there that my first theology course introduced me to documents of the Second Vatican Council and the admonition that "access to sacred Scripture ought to be open wide to the Christian faithful."[1] Still, it would take some time and study before I came to realize that the words on the sacred pages were addressed to me personally, leading me to know the Living Word of God—and that Catholicism was truly biblical.

On April 12, 1947, a Roman tram driver named Bruno Cornacchiola gained the same realization, albeit in a much more dramatic fashion and with the assistance of a heavenly visitor. He and his three children had planned an outing but they missed the train to Ostia, so they went instead to the Roman site known as Tre Fontane (Three Fountains), where St. Paul was believed to have been martyred. While the children played ball nearby, Bruno prepared a speech he was to give at a Seventh Day Adventist conference the next day, searching his Protestant Bible for proof that "Mary is neither ever Virgin nor immaculate."

Bruno was a lapsed Catholic who had found his way to Seventh Day Adventism after serving in the Spanish Civil War. He had developed an increasingly and fiercely militant hatred for the Catholic Church, even purchasing a dagger with which to murder Pope Pius XII. His devout Catholic spouse, Iolanda, desperate to dissuade him, asked him to make the nine First Fridays devotion to the Sacred Heart of Jesus, and he had done so. Nevertheless, that very morning, April 12, he had

---

1 "Dogmatic Constitution on Divine Revelation" (*Dei Verbum*), in *Vatican Council II: The Conciliar and Post Conciliar Documents*, ed. Austin Flannery (Liturgical Press, 1975), 22.

contemptuously written in pencil on the base of a statue of Mary, "You are neither virgin nor mother."

Absorbed in his speech preparations, Bruno was suddenly interrupted by one of his children who needed his help to search for their lost ball. He found his youngest son, Gianfranco, kneeling at the entrance to a dark cave, his eyes fixed in ecstatic prayer and repeating, "Beautiful lady! Beautiful lady!" Bruno was further confused and then terror-stricken to see his other two children falling to their knees in a similar manner, remaining motionless as though glued to the ground, and crying out together to the "beautiful lady."

What occurred next changed the entire course of Bruno's life. He was overwhelmed by a mystical experience of intense light and bodily weightlessness as an indescribably beautiful lady, dressed in a radiant white dress, a rose-colored sash, and a green mantle, appeared to him holding a small gray book clutched to her breast. She identified herself first as "one that is of the Divine Trinity"—daughter of the Father, mother of the Divine Son, and spouse of the Holy Spirit—and then added, "I am the Virgin of the Revelation."

She sternly reprimanded Bruno for persecuting her and revealed the sinful condition of his soul. She further commanded him to return to the Catholic Church, the "true sheepfold" and "pure source of the Gospel," and to renounce the errors which deemed her divinely given privileges as mere human inventions. She then begged for prayer—especially the daily Rosary—for the conversion of unbelievers, adding that she would perform powerful miracles for their restoration.

The lady also revealed a message which would have great significance for Marian dogma: "My body could not be allowed to decay. My Son came for me with His Angels." When Bruno later communicated this message to Pope Pius XII, he unwittingly provided the pontiff with confirmation for the dogma of the Assumption, which was solemnly declared a mere three years after the apparition.[2]

Although the site of the apparition at Tre Fontane has since drawn large numbers of pilgrims, and although Popes Pius XII and John Paul II favorably regarded its subsequent fruits of miraculous healings and conversions—not the least of which was Bruno's own miraculous conversion—the apparition of the Virgin of the Revelation has not yet received official approval. In fact, I had never even heard of it until a visit to Rome in 2021, when a friend took me to a site half hidden by a grove of trees adjoining a modest parking lot off the Via Laurentina. There was nothing physically imposing about it; in fact, one would hardly know that a Marian shrine was there. And yet, the presence of Our Lady was palpable.

I was fascinated by Bruno's story but even more stirred by the mementoes of miracles lining the walls of a dimly lit tunnel which marks the grotto of apparition. Marble plaques with names and dates are set into the mosaics and photographs are tucked into every crevice. In the main worship area—an open-sided, covered space with rows of simple folding chairs—a large statue of the Virgin of the Revelation invites visitors to pause for prayer and reflection. But I saw no structural grandeur to detract from the collective, uncomplicated testimony of faith. This is simply a place where Mary, mother and revealer of the Word made flesh, brings hope to the faithful, especially those desperate for the spiritual conversion and healing of their loved ones.

But why "Virgin of the Revelation"? And what was the significance of the gray book she clasped so tightly?

---

2   This historical account of the apparition and its aftermath is largely dependent upon two sources: "The History," Missionaries of Divine Revelation, http://mdrevelation.org/the-virgin-of-revelation/the-history/, and Benjamin Crockett, "Our Lady of the Revelation: The Message of Tre Fontane," EWTN Vatican, December 8, 2024, https://www.ewtnvatican.com/articles/our-lady-of-the-revelation-the-message-of-tre-fontane-3955. The latter also references the book by François Vayne, *The Virgin of Revelation: The Message of Tre Fontane*, originally published as *La Vierge de l'Apocalypse: Aux portes de Rome, les apparitions de Tre Fontane* (Artege, 2024).

That book was in fact the Bible, and her appearance at Tre Fontane was undoubtedly meant to stress that the revelation of her Son occurred not only in human flesh as delineated by time and space, but also as he is eternally revealed in the Sacred Scriptures that are handed down and taught through the Catholic Church. In this, Mary's message to Bruno was most emphatic. Although he had been studying the scriptures, he did so with blinded eyes and a hardened heart that was estranged and even hostile toward both the Mother of God and God's Church.

Although I was never overtly hostile toward Catholicism, I lived with a similar blindness and closed-heartedness for several years. While in my late teens, I jumped into Bible study with great enthusiasm but also with frustration and bitterness toward the church of my youth. Why had my Catholic religion teachers never taught me about the Bible—not the coffee table kind but the kind that I could read and understand? Why did I feel that I had to leave the Catholic Church in order to have a living, personal relationship with Jesus Christ? And what did Mary have to do with any of this, other than giving birth to the Savior?

Eventually I became so disenchanted with Catholicism that I began praying for the "conversion" of my family members and friends, hoping that they would awaken to a "true" Christianity that was biblically based. And I am chagrined to admit that I had little use for Mary at all.

I can't exactly pinpoint a moment when my doubt and antagonism toward the Catholic Church changed. Maybe it was the experience of being around other Catholics who actually loved reading the Bible and who understood it. Maybe it was a second theology course during a semester in Rome. Maybe it was meeting my husband—a devout Catholic man with a strong devotion to Our Lady—while in college. I only know that my resistance to being Catholic began to vanish, and I realized in my deepest self that I had returned not only to my spiritual home but to my spiritual Mother.

I wouldn't trade those teen years and my introduction to the Bible for anything. I am profoundly grateful for those evangelical Christian friends who opened my eyes to the depth and the meaning of Scripture and opened my heart to a Savior who died and rose for me. But I am also convinced that the teachings of the Catholic faith are rooted firmly in Scripture and that reading the Bible through a Catholic lens is a sure path to knowing Jesus as the Way, the Truth, and the Life.

There are times in all our lives when we might be more like Bruno Cornacchiola than we realize. We seek to rationalize or even twist the teachings of our Catholic faith for our own selfish purposes and agendas, even to the point of hostility toward those who reveal to us the truth we'd rather not see or hear. No matter what blindness may hold us bound, we can turn humbly to the Virgin of the Revelation, who is always ready to lead us away from error and guide us toward the saving love of her Son.

Sharon K. Perkins, M.A., is a forty-five-year veteran of Catholic parish and diocesan catechetical ministry who is now enjoying "retirement" by freelance speaking, writing, serving on Catholic boards, and playing with her two grandsons. She and her husband, Mike, have been married forty-seven years and live in North Texas. You can find her at *sharonkperkins.com*.

XXIII

Queen of Peace

How Mary Teaches Us to Pray

Christine Rich

*I am coming among you because I desire to
be your mother—your intercessor.*[1]

—Medjugorje, March 18, 2012

"Do you know that you have a true mother in heaven who loves you far more than your earthly mother, and she wants to care for you in a tangible way?"

I was thirty-two years old when I heard a priest ask this question at my nephew's First Communion Mass. I had been born and raised Catholic and I believed in Mary, but I had never thought of her as my true mother, or as the true mother of my own children.

At that time, I had been suffering for almost four years with anxiety and worry for my son, whom we had started in kindergarten before he turned five. I had regretted that decision ever since, but no one would agree with me that it would be good for him to repeat a year in school.

---

1 Mirjana Soldo, *My Heart Will Triumph* (Cocoa, FL: CatholicShop Publishing), 15.

Now, hearing the words of that faithful priest, I knew that Mary felt my pain.

Before bed that night I prayed, "Mary, if my son is your true son, I give him to you and I ask you to please take care of him. I will say one Hail Mary every night as intercession for this petition."

I am still embarrassed to this day for the meager offering I made, but she was not offended by it. In fact, within one week my son's teacher asked to meet with me and sheepishly suggested that, although he was a sweet and smart boy, she didn't feel that he fit in with his current peers. She believed that giving him the gift to repeat third grade might be the best thing for him.

I cried both in sorrow and joy. I cried in sorrow for the pain this would bring my young son and in joy because my prayer had been answered in such a short time. She interceded to save my son (and me) from great suffering. And in doing so, she brought *peace* to the heart of a young boy and his mother.

Mary, the mother of Jesus, "the Prince of Peace" (Isaiah 9:6), is venerated as Queen of Peace because she is our intercessor for peace, and she teaches us how to live in the abiding peace of her Son. The origins of the title Queen of Peace date back at least to the sixteenth century in France.[2] It was formally added to the Litany of Loreto by Pope Benedict XV on May 3, 1917, during World War I, to invoke Mary's help in bringing an end to the conflict. Just eight days later, Our Lady appeared to three children in Fatima and instructed them to pray the Rosary for peace in the world.[3]

This Marian title has more recently gained prominence through the spiritual phenomena reported in Medjugorje, Bosnia and Herzegovina,

---

2 Bulletin message, "History of the Marian Title: Queen of Peace," Our Lady Queen of Peace R.C. Church, https://olqpbranchville.org/about-the-marian-title-queen-of-peace.

3 Fr. Donald Calloway, "The Original Final Invocations of the Litany," Marians of the Immaculate Conception, February 9, 2020, https://marian.org/articles/original-final-invocations-litany.

where six young people are said to have begun receiving apparitions of Mary in 1981. In these visions, she has identified herself as the Queen of Peace. Here, our Blessed Mother reportedly told one of the visionaries, Mirjana (Dragicevic) Soldo, "What I started in Fatima, I will finish in Medjugorje. My heart will triumph."[4]

While the apparitions in Medjugorje have not yet been officially approved by the Church, in 2024 the Vatican released a document authorizing the granting of a *nihil obstat* ("nothing obstructs") for the phenomena. The *nihil obstat,* without expressing any certainty about the supernatural authenticity of the phenomenon itself, acknowledges many signs of the actions of the Holy Spirit "in the midst" of a given spiritual experience.[5]

I traveled to Medjugorje for the first time in 2009. I had read everything I could get my hands on about this little town in Bosnia and Herzegovina in Eastern Europe. I was giddy with excitement because after all of my research I was determined that I would see Our Blessed Mother on the mountain there!

But I was a little disappointed when we arrived in Medjugorje. It had been described as a piece of heaven, but I had pictured heaven to be much more beautiful than this place. In just a short time there, however, I realized my mistake. Medjugorje was not a *piece* of heaven, but it's a place where one can experience the *peace* of heaven.

Heaven seeps in. When you step off the bus into Medjugorje, you experience heaven. Why? Because of the worship. All the sacrifices, the penances, the rosaries, the adoration hours, the praise and worship, and especially all the Holy Masses being offered—all this worship of God

---

4   Mirjana Soldo, *My Heart Will Triumph* (Cocoa, FL: CatholicShop Publishing), 145.

5   Jimmy Akin, "Medjugorje, A Closer Look at the Vatican's Cautious Ruling," *National Catholic Register,* September 20, 2024, https://www.ncregister.com/commentaries/medjugorje-closer-look-at-vatican-ruling.

results in God pouring down his graces and blessings for sanctification and holiness.[6]

And the pilgrims who flock to Medjugorje get to step right into it. We step into the river of peace created there by the "school of prayer" that our Blessed Mother teaches in her messages to the world. She reportedly conveys that she has been given a time of special grace by the Father in heaven to help all of her children get to heaven. And when she refers to her "children," she says she is speaking of all people of the world.

Mary has been said to ask for the simple, yet powerful, tasks of daily prayer with the Holy Bible, attendance at Mass every Sunday and more often if possible, praying the Rosary daily, and choosing to fast on Wednesdays and Fridays. She is also adamant when it comes to the value of monthly confession. In fact, one of the nicknames that has been given to Medjugorje is "the confessional of the world." In confession the layers of sin are peeled off, and we become fully the children of God he created us to be. We come to understand who and what we are made for once we have the courage to step off the boat (or bus) and into the water.

In two short days on my first visit there, I participated as fully as possible in the daily faith program that is promoted there. I cried when I left and prayed I would be able to go back one day. I had been profoundly changed. To stay close to Mary when I returned home, I continued to read and pray with a book that contained the messages that she is said to have shared in Medjugorje.

Her very first message to the children was simple: "Peace, peace, peace and only peace! Peace must reign between God and men, and between all men."[7] I was intrigued by this message and wanted to know more because when I returned home, I was not feeling peace in my heart. I wanted what Jesus had given to his disciples when he told them, "Peace I leave you; my peace I give to you" (John 14:27). So I took my anxieties to confession

---

6 Fr. Matt Williams, "Lord, what are You doing to me? You're ruining my life, Lord," Caritas of Birmingham, August 19, 2009, https://medjugorje.com/lord-what-are-you-doing-to-me/.

7 Soldo, *My Heart Will Triumph*, 42.

one day, and the priest asked me a question that had never been posed to me before: "How is your prayer life?" I told him I wasn't sure how to answer that question because I did not know what a prayer life was or what it looked like to live one out.

This sent me on a quest, and the Queen of Peace walked right alongside me back to Medjugorje. By the grace of God, the Catholic jewelry company that I had co-founded started having our jewelry pieces hand-woven by women in Medjugorje. I was the liaison between the women in Medjugorje and our company, which took me back to this very special place at least once a year.

On one trip there I was sitting in the adoration chapel pleading with Jesus for help with many things when I heard an interior voice say very quietly, "It's all about prayer."

I sat contemplating this, feeling like Martha, "worried and distracted by many things" (Luke 10:41). Yet it was as if I got to watch a movie of Jesus in the scene with Martha. When he said this to her, he was kind and gentle and looked at her with such love in his eyes. It was as if he was telling her so much more than the spoken words could convey.

His eyes told of how he knew Martha's heart. He knew how much she loved and cared for her brother and sister. He knew all the pressure she was under to run a household because her brother, Lazarus, was sick. He knew all the ups and downs of her relationship with her sister, Mary, who now sat at his feet. And his eyes told Martha how much he loved her and how greatly he desired for her to love him.

At the same time, his eyes told me how much he loved me and how greatly he desired for me to love him.

And then he gave the answer to everything: choose "the better part, which will not be taken away" (Luke 10:42). This is what Martha's sister, Mary, had done. She sat at the feet of Jesus and *listened* to him, coming to know him and to recognize his voice.

This is what Jesus' mother had done for thirty years. She sat at his feet and listened to all he had to share about the will of the Father, and she served him with great love. And it is what his mother wants to teach us. The messages of Medjugorje remind the faithful that we need to pray, to sit at the feet of her Son every day and let him transform our hearts.

The visionary Mirjana has shared, "I believe that if Our Lady had to use just one word to answer every question ever asked of her, it would probably be 'Pray'. Our prayers, she (Our Lady) says, have the power to change everything."[8]

One of the prevailing characteristics of the spirituality that emerges from the messages in Medjugorje is that of trust in God through a total trust in Mary, in order to become instruments of peace in the world.[9] In fact, her latest public message at the time of this writing was short and simple: "Dear children! May this time for you be a time of prayer for peace."[10]

Prayer allows for small conversions of heart that are the conduit through which Jesus pours out peace into each heart that will allow peace to reign "between God and men and between all men"!

Here are a few simple practices I have learned from the Queen of Peace that have helped me develop a prayer life:

- Before I even open my eyes each morning, I pray the Memorare to ask Mary to walk with me and guide me to stay close to Jesus throughout the day.
- I make time each morning to pray with the daily gospel and listen to what Jesus would like to share with me about my own heart and my day ahead.
- I look forward to Sunday Mass each week and daily Mass as often as I am able to attend.

---

8   Ibid., 264.

9   "History of the Marian Title: Queen of Peace."

10 "Message From Our Lady," Mary TV Medjugorje, September 25, 2025, https://marytv.tv/messages-from-our-lady/.

- I prioritize getting to confession once a month and relish the freedom and healing I receive each time.
- I pray a Rosary daily, walking with our Blessed Mother through the life of her Son.

Mary brought peace into my heart when I was a young mother, responding with great generosity to my meager offering of just a few Hail Marys, and since then she has patiently led me to the deeper peace that her Son has promised each one of us. I now understand more fully what that interior voice said to me over a decade ago in adoration, "It's all about prayer." *Peace* is developed and deepened through a life of prayer.

By the way, my little boy whom I had worried so much about is now a young adult, who was the first to receive a college diploma in the long line of men on his father's side of the family. He is married to a beautiful young woman, and they currently have two precious and rambunctious toddlers. I pray Mary continues to mother him and leads him to the abiding peace of her Son.

Our Mother, Queen of Peace, pray for us.

Through mentoring, writing, and leading pilgrimages, **Christine Rich** is passionate about walking with souls on their journey with God. Christine founded the Imfura Foundation to share the messages of Our Blessed Mother from around the world, promoting forgiveness, healing, and unity through the power of prayer. Go to *imfura.com/pray* for a free pdf of the "40 Day Prayer Pledge" for a jumpstart in creating a habit of prayer.

XXVI

Our Lady of Las Lajas

How Mary Intercedes for Our Reconciliation and Healing

Anna Smit

From now on, therefore, we regard no one from a human point of view; even though we once knew Christ from a human point of view, we know him no longer in that way.

—2 Corinthians 5:16

Ascene in Helen Keller's autobiography, *The Complete Story of My Life*, touched me deeply as a child. Helen, who became deaf, mute, and blind at nineteen months old, describes the moment when what had been a dead word for her suddenly became a "living word."[1] Her private tutor, Annie Sullivan, took Helen to a well where someone was drawing out water. Annie let that water gush out into Helen's hand as she wrote the word *water* in the palm of her pupil's other hand.

Moments after this great awakening, Helen remembered something hurtful she had just done and began weeping in godly sorrow. The eyes of her heart, which had been shut tight in distrust and rebellion, suddenly

---

1   Helen Keller, *The Complete Story of My Life* (Orinda, CA: SeaWolf Press, 2020), 16–18.

opened wide. In God's kindness to her, through her teacher's intercession, she was led to repentance.

What lingered with me as a child was Annie's response to Helen's rebellion. Right before this beautiful scene at the well took place, Helen had thrown a gift Annie had given her, a handmade doll, onto the floor, breaking it, as she boiled over with anger and frustration. Yet despite the pain this must have caused her, Annie chose not to reprimand Helen.

She chose instead to focus on the pain of her pupil, a pain she most likely understood was at the root of Helen's hurtful actions. And so, rather than treat the symptom by correcting her behavior, she went to the root of her rebellion: the heartache caused by Helen's inability to communicate with the world around her. Annie chose to meet Helen's anger and rebellion with loving perseverance. She tirelessly attempted to restore her pupil's ability to communicate, a restoration which would also open Helen's spiritual eyes and ears to God's love for her.

All this came to mind again recently, as I learned about the not-so-well-known apparition of the Blessed Mother and the child Jesus in Colombia, Our Lady of Las Lajas (Our Lady of the Rocks). I saw parallels between these two true stories, both of which show the miracle-working power of the Living Word in the intercession of a gentle-hearted woman. I also saw a connection between these stories and my own experience of God's healing through the Blessed Mother's intercession.

The story of this little known apparition began in 1754, in a cave in Colombia, after the sudden onset of a terrible storm. A mother, María Mueses de Quiñones, took shelter there with her young daughter, Rosa, a small child who was deaf and mute. The cave was rumored to be haunted, and María felt afraid, so she invoked the protection of the Virgin of the Rosary. Suddenly, she felt someone tap her shoulder, which frightened her into flight, clutching her daughter close to her chest as she ran.

A few days later, María was forced to walk back toward that same cave, as it was the only way to get herself and her daughter home safely. As she sat to rest on a rock near the cave, she let Rosa go off to play.

Moments later, she was astounded to hear her mute daughter calling, "Mommy, there is a woman in here with a boy in her arms!"[2] Terrified by this miracle, María again ran away, clutching her daughter.

Days later, Rosa suddenly disappeared. María immediately knew where to look for her: in that same cave. Arriving there, she saw Rosa kneeling before a regal woman. This woman had let her young son down from her lap to play with Rosa. María recognized this woman as the Blessed Mother and her son as Jesus, the Son of God. Fearful of being ridiculed and not believed, however, she decided to tell no one about it.

Some time later, Rosa died. In the depths of her sorrow, María took the body of her little girl back to the cave to seek the Blessed Mother's intercession. Deeply moved by the mother's sorrow, Our Lady intervened, praying for Rosa, and the girl came to life again. This time, María spoke freely of the apparition and all that Mary had done for her.

Later, an incredible image was found on a rock at the site of the apparition. The image portrays Our Lady holding her child and giving St. Dominic a rosary, while the child Jesus hands a friar's cord to St. Francis of Assisi. In testing the image, scientists discovered it was part of the rock itself and could not have been made by man. The colors even reach several feet deep into the rock's crust. Consequently, the Catholic Church sanctioned devotion to Our Lady of Las Lajas (Our Lady of the Rocks) in 1951, and the church that was built around the image has been declared a minor basilica.[3]

What struck me, both in this apparition and the story of Helen Keller, is how love can seem frightening at first. We see it in María running from Mary's touch. We see it in Helen throwing Annie Sullivan's sweet gift to the floor and breaking it. I see it in my own continuing journey of

---

2   John Carpenter, "Marian Apparitions: Our Lady of Las Lajas, Colombia, 1754," *Divine Mysteries and Miracles*, July 23, 2016, www.divinemysteries.info/our-lady-of-las-lajas-colombia-1754.

3   Fr. Donald Colloway, "The Miraculous Image of Our Lady of Las Lajas," *Catholic Exchange*, March 29, 2017, www.catholicexchange.com/miraculous-image-lady-las-lajas/.

conversion, in each step I have taken toward the Blessed Mother and the thoughts of terror that flooded my mind, rooted in my Protestant past.

But it's also beautiful to see how God met María and Helen in their fears, and to reflect upon how he has been meeting me in my fears as well. You see, the Blessed Mother was the biggest obstacle on my path to conversion. Yet, as in the case of María, to get home safely, I knew I had to "pass by the cave"—I had to draw near to her in spite of my fears.

Much like María, I sat on the rock, resting in God's presence through his Church, but not venturing closer to Mary, the Mother of that Church. I called upon her intercession, praying the Rosary daily (with some trepidation). But it took the Lord setting others before me, who spoke to me of Mary and Jesus, to open my heart to receive God's love for me through her.

Before my conversion, I remember being so concerned about doing the wrong thing in seeking Mary that I cried out in prayer, asking God to make his will blatantly obvious to me. Soon after, a woman from Rwanda reached out to me in the parking lot of my parish. As we lingered, getting to know each other, this woman, without knowing about my prayer, told me all about the apparitions in her home country, in which the Blessed Mother urged the people of Rwanda to draw near to Christ in repentance. I was awestruck by what she shared and promptly ordered a book about it, which gently pried open my heart.

Soon after that, I consecrated myself to Jesus through Mary, again experiencing God's consolation through others, as anxious thoughts multiplied within me. Then one day during Eucharistic adoration, after my conversion, I was praying the Rosary before the Blessed Sacrament when a wound from my childhood came to mind. In that memory, I found Mary pouring out her motherly love and affection over me, and through her prayers I felt the Holy Spirit acknowledge the deep pain that wounding had caused me.

Then another memory surfaced—a memory of how I had wounded the very person who had once wounded me. Yet as I wanted to recoil in shame, Mary again poured out her motherly love and affection upon me. I found the Holy Spirit acknowledging the deep pain beneath my shame: the pain of having wounded my loved one. Through Mary's intercession, my eyes also opened to notice something I hadn't before: how not just I, but also the person I had wounded, had found ourselves frozen in those moments we had wanted to come to each other's aid.

As a child, I was given the gift of seeing and loving a traumatized loved one through God's eyes of mercy, as Annie had Helen. But in suffering rejection for doing so, I decided to hide my godly convictions to remain "safe". Eventually, I even denied Christ outright, by embracing a lie the enemy fed me, as truth. Ironically, I decided that disobeying man's authority to follow my (godly) convictions (Christ in me) was the same as disobeying God.

I had come to understand how agreeing with this lie shackled my body into adulthood, freezing me in moments I wanted to speak up in love, but I had never stopped to consider that this might also apply to my loved one. As I recalled the merciful love she had expressed throughout her life, I now realized how much pain it must have caused her to withhold that love. Now, in feeling my own pain and sorrow at not having come to her aid, I was able to receive her love for me in the moments I now realized she too had so longed to come to my aid.

As I prayed the Rosary that day, it was as if Mary had taken hold of my hands and poured out the living water of God's Word into one hand and the revelation of his Word in the other. She had set the child Jesus before me, revealing his presence in myself and in my loved one. This empowered me to bring my wounding of my loved one to the Sacrament of Reconciliation where Jesus showered me with even more grace.

Months after that confession, I stood before a sculpture of the Blessed Mother holding the crucified Jesus in her arms, and I looked intently into her tear-strained eyes. I felt my heart being filled with overwhelming pain and sorrow, as if the Holy Spirit was giving me a small taste of the Blessed Mother's cup of anguish. Yet in that anguish I also felt the depths of her love and mercy pouring into me. This helped me see that Mary's fiat to a cross of suffering had also been her yes to a cross of ever deepening love for us.

It reminded me of kissing the nail-pierced feet of Jesus on a crucifix on my first Good Friday in a Catholic parish. I was overcome by that same anguish and unfathomably deep love of Christ for us all in our sin. Now, standing before that sculpture of Mary, my eyes were opened to the union of Mary's and Christ's hearts, as I felt God extend me an invitation to come to know his heart better by drawing nearer to his mother.

As I did so, I was given the grace to see how I still clung to my loved one's wounding of me, blaming that experience for my struggle to trust God. Suddenly, I realized that by doing so, I was choosing to reject God's healing by walking in unforgiveness. After bringing this to confession, I realized I now have a beautiful way to grow in my trust of God: by repeatedly calling to mind Christ's love and his healing and forgiveness of us both.

As I take note of these various details of my journey homeward, I cannot help but wonder if Our Lady of Las Lajas was already interceding for me long before I knew her. By placing little Jesus before them and praying for them, Mary brought María and Rosa the grace they needed to hear, see, and open their mouths to speak—a grace I recognize in my own story.

Just as Annie loved Helen in her brokenness and pain, I can now see how Mary was not just interceding for me to recognize Christ's heart in my loved one, but also to affirm his heart of mercy in me as a child. The apparition of Our Lady of the Rocks encourages me to abide in that merciful heart, to set the little child Jesus before others by loving them as Christ has loved me, just as Mary did for me.

Our Lady of Las Lajas, pray for us to see and receive Christ in ourselves and in each other. Pray that we may become messengers of reconciliation in receiving God's forgiveness and forgiving others, as Christ has forgiven us.

Anna Smit grew up as a missionary and pastor's kid, but chose to deny and turn her back on Christ in her teens. After a long (continuing) journey of conversion, she followed the Holy Spirit's call into the Catholic Church. Here, God has been fulfilling the desires of her eleven year old heart: to know Him in the depths of His grace. You can read more of her writing at *allshallknowme.substack.com.*

XXV

Handmaid of the Lord

How Mary Teaches Us to Accept God's Will in All Things

Ruth Ellen Naef

Then Mary said, "Here am I, the servant of the Lord;
let it be with me according to your word."

—Luke 1:38

"Forever, you will be handmaids of the Handmaid of the Lord."
A holy woman spoke these prophetic words to my friend Tina and me. We were home from work on disability at the same time. Soon each of us would be diagnosed with a different neuromuscular disease.

I was home after having my first stroke-like episode caused by a mitochondrial disease, a rare disorder that depletes my energy, affecting my brain and muscles. The exhaustion that sets in from what most would consider minimal daily activity sets off an array of symptoms. When these flares come, I am totally dependent on others.

Tina received worse news: a fatal diagnosis of Amyotrophic Lateral Sclerosis (ALS).

We prayed for a miracle for Tina, but she didn't receive physical healing. Rather, she was totally transformed into a handmaid of Mary. This took place in front of my eyes. Like Mary and Jesus, Tina accepted the will of the Father without complaint. She had a total trust in Jesus, particularly in dying to her vocation of wife and mother to her family on earth. She surrendered her husband and two children into the hands of Jesus. After she passed, I saw how Jesus brought two mourning families together to become one, as Tina's husband met and married a widow who had tragically lost her first husband to ALS. And they thrived.

Unlike Tina, my transformation into a true handmaid of Mary wouldn't come until about twenty-five years later. And even now, I continue on the path of transformation.

"Handmaid of the Lord" is the way Mary describes herself at the Annunciation. This moment is so important that Catholics have traditionally commemorated it by praying the Angelus at six a.m., noon, and six p.m. each day, reciting:

> *V/. Behold the handmaid of the Lord.*
> *R/. Be it done unto me according to your word.*

In the moment of the Annunciation, Mary already fulfilled what Jesus would teach his disciples in the Our Father: to accept the Father's will in all things (see Matthew 6:10).

A handmaid was typically a servant with the lowest position in the household, taking orders from her mistress.[1] When Mary calls herself God's handmaid, she shows that she understands herself to be both blessed in becoming the mother of our Savior, and of low estate, as she says in her Magnificat:

> My soul magnifies the Lord,
> and my spirit rejoices in God my Savior,
> for he has looked on the lowliness of his servant.
> Surely, from now on all generations will call me blessed;
> for the Mighty One has done great things for me,

---

1   Pat Marrin, "Handmaid of the Lord," *National Catholic Reporter*, December 19, 2019, https://www.ncronline.org/spirituality/pencil-preaching/pencil-preaching/handmaid-lord.

and holy is his name. (Luke 1:46–48)

Mary attributes everything to God. She understands that even her humility is a gift from God, and she chooses to accept the will of the Father in all things. Mary dies to any plans she may have had for her own life. Her fiat is her total surrender. Perhaps as she spoke to the angel, she remembered the words of the prophet Jeremiah:"For surely I know the plans I have for you, says the Lord, plans for welfare and not for harm, to give you a future and a hope" (29:11).

Our hope, our Savior, came into the world through Mary in ways nobody could have anticipated. The King of Kings was born in a cave with animals. His crib was a feeding trough. The messiah was unwelcome at the inns of Bethlehem while all of Israel was eagerly awaiting his coming.

There's so much contradiction between God's plans and the plans of the world. Earthly desires are for self-comfort and self-interest. Yet God himself chose to suffer the ailments his creatures encounter in life. And Jesus invited his mother to join him in suffering for the life of the world. Mary replied yes to the will of the Father, accepting that his plans are for good, and as we strive to imitate her, we grow to do the Father's will better.

We too are called to be in union with God, wanting to do his will. We cannot do this without always giving our yes to what God asks of us. Who of us can say we do this well? Yet we should continually strive to do better in imitating Jesus and Mary.

We are called to be disciples of Jesus. And if we are true disciples, we will do what he asked us to do: "I give you a new commandment, that you love one another. Just as I have loved you, you also should love one another" (John 13:34). Jesus loved us to his death. In the same way, we are to love each other by dying to our own will and rising to do the will of the Father.

Thankfully, we do not journey alone. At the foot of the Cross, Jesus gave us his mother to be our mother, and to spiritually birth Jesus into our hearts in a more fervent way.

After I was home full time, I started going to daily Mass. At church we prayed the Rosary, and I would stay afterwards, learning to listen to Jesus in the tabernacle. I was growing closer to him. Still, there was something missing that I didn't understand. As my children grew older and life became busier, I fell away from these good spiritual practices. No longer did I pray the Rosary frequently, go to daily Mass, or sit in adoration. My faith became weaker. What was missing in my life? After all, I thought I was being a faithful Catholic.

My health declined. I was now in a hospital bed in my living room. Since I was homebound, my husband encouraged me to go to Sunday Mass again. It was difficult, but rewarding. Returning on Sundays helped me desire to grow in faith again. And my health, though still poor, improved.

Technology allowed me to further my studies in the Faith. I joined the online apostolate Women of Grace, where I found resources and holy friendships. My spiritual life grew. I now understood how important it is to grow closer to God in daily prayer, meditation, contemplation, and study. Here, I found the missing piece: a relationship not only with our God, but also with Mary.

Meditating daily on the mysteries of the Rosary, I saw everything from Jesus' perspective. I also prayed the Seven Sorrows Rosary, reflecting on the events in Jesus' life from Mary's point of view. I came to know each better. Now, before prayer, I ask Mary to bring me to Jesus.

While meditating on the mysteries, Jesus graced me with the gift of contemplative prayer. He gave me many sweet consolations. There were times I was so aware of his spiritual presence, I could almost reach out and touch him. Jesus helped me to climb Jacob's ladder in my spiritual growth. God is so good!

But in spiritual marriage, just as in an earthly marriage, the newlywed period comes to an end and real life begins. That is when the marriage is tested. At first, there are things we don't know about our spouse, and some bad habits make us irritable. *We never go out to dinner and see a show anymore. He never brings me flowers.* In the spiritual life also, at a certain point Jesus stops his sweet consolations. Our faith is tested. Will we still cling to him when he doesn't draw us in with those happy moments? Only a true love between ourselves and God can withstand the test. If we want to be in total union, we need to persevere, growing to love as God loves.

One way to keep growing spiritually is to keep the holy practices we've been doing when we don't feel God near us. We cling to the promise he gave us that he'll never abandon us. We have to believe this no matter the circumstances we face. Sorrow comes when we cannot seem to find him, yet we need to be joyful. He is testing us so we grow in faith. St. John of the Cross calls this the dark night of the senses. In these times we experience both spiritual dryness and moments when we sense God's presence.

As we walk through these challenges, Mary teaches us to be more humble. It was through the gift of self-awareness that I saw my pride, and God worked through a holy priest to confirm this. Then I was invited to do a consecration to Jesus through Mary.

St. Louis de Montfort says we should be holy slaves to Mary. During my consecration, I found that this is how I was to become a handmaid of the Handmaid of the Lord: I needed to truly become aware of Mary's work in my life.

In living my consecration, I found it necessary to be humble myself. I knew my relationship with Jesus would never be as close as his with Mary, and that her intercession is so much greater than mine. Accepting these truths showed me that Mary became the person God created her to be. In the same way, Ruth Ellen has to become the person God created me to be. Striving to imitate Mary's humility and her generous yes to the will of the Father was the perfect way to start my journey toward humility and accepting the will of the Father in every circumstance.

Suffering is part of the mission for each of us. People will often tell me they couldn't bear my cross. And that's just it. This is my cross, and I couldn't bear another's either. The best we can do is offer our sufferings and pray for others that they may bear their crosses well. In this way, we make it easier for each other in hope that all will grow closer to God as he transforms us. And because we know that Jesus' passion, death, and resurrection brought new life, we like St. Paul (see Colossians 1:24) can rejoice in our suffering for the sake of the body of Christ.

Joy and suffering can occur simultaneously. We see this in Mary's life, as the Presentation and Finding Jesus in the Temple are both in the Joyful Mysteries of the Rosary and counted among Our Lady's seven sorrows. We also see these things in our daily lives. For example, there's joy in a graduation or a wedding day, and yet a parent who has died is not present. Even if both parents are alive to celebrate this joyful event, they can experience a real sorrow in letting go, as their children mature into a life of independence. Recently, I have encountered this reality in my own life.

As I write this, I sit in my motorized wheelchair as a patient in a rehabilitation hospital. I've been hospitalized twice in a month due to a virus that flared my disease. My neuropathy and migraines have become worse, and it's more difficult to walk with a walker. My endurance has become minimal. As I go through these flares, I find it easier to accept them. It isn't that I like the pain or incapacities. I don't like them at all. But I have found we can all offer up to God both small and heavy burdens. We also receive joy in the knowledge that God is using all our sufferings. And if we can help but one soul, it's all worth it. I know I am nothing without God, and he allows these ailments as a gift to help others. He also transforms me as I find peace even in these storms, knowing it is God who strengthens me.

I used to think I was good. Now, like Mary, I know that it is God who is the goodness within me. I strive to keep growing in him. I know I'm not perfect; it is God who perfects me. Thank you, Mary. And may I strive to be forever a handmaid of the Handmaid of the Lord.

Knowing that we are called to an ongoing, deepening conversion, **Ruth Ellen Naef** believes that suffering can be an opportunity to grow in our relationship with God. Ruth Ellen is a cradle Catholic, a wife of thirty-eight years, and a mother of two. This is her second collaborative writing project with the Praise Writers Community. You can follow her on Facebook *@ Ruth Ellen Naef.*

XXVI

OUR LADY OF LOURDES

Becoming a Pilgrim of Hope

Frances Smit

*For in hope we were saved. Now hope that sees for itself
is not hope. For who hopes for what one sees?*

—Romans 8:24

"It's a miracle of Lourdes!" I exclaimed.

Her eyes narrowed as if in suspicion. "No, it's not."

Her expression said it all. *I don't believe in such things.*

After we had drunk and lathered ourselves with the healing water at the Lourdes baths, my sister's husband phoned out of the blue from the United States. The special medication she had been awaiting for over two months—the one that was supposed to be backordered for another umpteen months—had just come in.

I saw it as a miracle brought about Our Lady's intercession.

She didn't.

I felt a gulf between me and my unbelieving sister.

My sister had shed tears during the Lourdes bath. I imagined Our Lady bathing her with comfort in her recent medical diagnosis, painful marriage, and sick child. Yet her response to my exclamation reinforced what I already knew: she was not a pilgrim, but a tourist. Even if she's an unbeliever, a diehard tourist does the water gesture when she's at Lourdes.

I got my hopes up when I managed to cajole her into joining me in a trip to Lourdes. Why did I invite my unbelieving sister to Lourdes? Because, despite everything, I dared, even if foolishly, to hope. To love someone is to want the best for them. I wanted to bring my sister to Our Lady, to give her the very best, not only physically, but spiritually, so I threw my "pearls" (see Matthew 7:6), and she did not receive them.[1]

Now I slumped to the ground to pick up the pearls of my expectations off the floor. I tried to remember that God hears our prayers despite all appearances, and I put on my big girl trust pants.

While waiting to enter the Lourdes baths, hopefuls sit on benches that face the entrance. The *malades* (French word for the ill) in wheelchairs get priority in a special spot at the front of the line. They sit front and center, in the line of vision of the non-wheelchair-bound pilgrims. I couldn't help but watch them while I waited for our turn.

Each *malade* has a designated volunteer from the Order of Malta, a personal wheelchair driver and assistant. With their signature ascot scarves and blue vests, volunteers come from all over the world to get matched up with a *malade* by common language and other criteria.

As we inched closer to the entrance to the baths, I noticed one volunteer in particular. He sat with a wheelchair-bound lady who stared blankly ahead, motionless, as though she were asleep with her eyes open. In contrast to her, the volunteer was animated and lively. Though his

---

1 Pope Benedict XVI says in his encyclical, *Caritas in Veritate* (charity in truth), "Only in truth does charity shine forth, only in truth can charity be authentically lived. Truth is the light that gives meaning and value to charity. That light is both the light of reason and the light of faith, through which the intellect attains to the natural and supernatural truth of charity: it grasps its meaning as gift, acceptance, and communion." We do not think of our non-believing family members as swine, and that is not the point I'm trying to make here. But they cannot accept the gift of truth in its fullness because they see with the light of reason but not the light of faith. https://www.vatican.va/content/benedict-xvi/en/encyclicals/documents/hf_ben-xvi_enc_20090629_caritas-in-veritate.html.

malade gave no response, he enthusiastically monologued as her personal cheerleader.

He unsheathed a handheld fan from his bag of goodies to cool her in the July heat that would make even a lizard scramble for shade. Then he pulled out a water bottle and gently held it for her to drink. All the while, he resumed lilting cheerfully to the unresponsive, slightly slumped lady.

I was struck by his doting attention. At the same time, my sister, sitting beside me, had chattered nonstop. I pulled out my sweaty water bottle and took a break from the dual attentions needed to both listen and pray.

Soon after, I realized that my sister was my *malade*—physically ill and spiritually asleep. In turn, I would become hers—one whose hope had been dashed but who must hope on.

You can lead a horse to water but you can't make her drink (though she did drink the Lourdes water—just saying). One keeps hoping and praying, and then leaves the rest up to the Almighty.

For my sister's part, she lit candles with me and accompanied me to the evening torchlight procession. As the drizzling rain dusted our hair and eyelashes with dew, we watched the procession of pilgrims, which fills many city blocks, carry their lights and recite the Rosary. She even admitted, "I can see how this would be exciting for a Catholic."

To make her experience there the best it could be, miracle or no miracle, I morphed into her personal tour server. I let her pick every restaurant where we ate, every type of food. She wanted croissants so we ordered them, even though butter cramps my stomach and gluten bloats my middle like the blueberry girl in Willy Wonka.

She wanted French coffee and baguettes, so we went to a café where we bathed our nose hairs and palates in the aroma of fresh coffee and bread. She wanted crepes, so I used up my phone data allowance to find a 4+ star place. I thought if she enjoyed her experience at Lourdes, the place associated with Our Lady, then she might one day be open to her.

My sister is ever directionally challenged and so am I. Since my phone navigation app decided to speak only in French and otherwise proved unreliable, I studied maps into the night, memorizing street names and turns. Thus I served as navigator to show her places she might enjoy. I researched nature adventures, took her to an authentic French food market, and exchanged currency for her using my broken French.

I held up the Grotto of Massabielle line so she could snap and re-snap a photo of me to her liking, while silently apologizing to the pilgrims who prayed the Rosary and observed the tourist spectacle that was us.

I led her through narrow streets with luggage wheels clicking, dodging zipping cars to the train station so she wouldn't get lost and could catch her train on time. When it was over, I collapsed onto the guesthouse loft bed.

Everyone who loves a nonbeliever, a wayward, a prodigal, belongs to a club for which we didn't sign up. The yearning to be together with them in faith and truth, like the common bloodline we share, is a pulsating, parched thirst.

Sometimes our precious pearls come out before we even realize what we are doing or who is standing before us. When they eyeball our naked, exposed pearls (and even us) with suspicion, we have set ourselves up for the trample. Even if we knew this might be the outcome, we wander around dazed, dejected, and clutching our pearls.

Yet how often are we so focused on our wayward family members that we miss others, not in our bloodlines, who, instead of narrowed eyes of suspicion, would widen them with joy at the sight of our pearls?

If we met a stranger, without the face of a sister or a loved one, would we be too fixated on those who reject our faith to pull out our pearls for them?

Since the Church approved the Marian apparitions at Lourdes in 1862, millions of suffering hopefuls have journeyed on pilgrimage to the site, tucked along the Pyrenees Mountains in southern France. There Our Lady appeared to fourteen-year-old Bernadette Soubirous eighteen times, from February 11 to July 16, 1858.

In one of those apparitions, Our Lady instructed Bernadette to drink from the fountain at the grotto. Seeing no fountain there, Bernadette dug and scratched at the gravel until water bubbled forth. All these years later, the spring continues to flow. The healing properties of the water at Lourdes are renowned, and millions of hopefuls seeking healing have flocked there.

Miraculous healings are submitted to the Lourdes Medical Bureau for authentication. Of the 7,000 claims of healing submitted, the Bureau has approved seventy-two as miraculous.[2]

I imagine one reason for the small handful of approvals is that physical healing can be proven and seen, but spiritual and emotional healing cannot. There are surely many more pilgrims who have been healed spiritually or emotionally, but those can't be counted as official.

An article about Lourdes popped up in my news feed. Its gist was that the true miracle of Lourdes is not receiving what is asked for but the grace to persevere in hope. Accepting the outcome and keeping hope alive *is* the miracle.

After my sister departed for her next tourist destination, I stayed at Lourdes for another day. As I sat alone on the edge of the Gave River, opposite the grotto, I noticed every pilgrim came with a group. Some displayed their togetherness with matching outfits and waving flags. Many of these groups were led by priests who headed up their throng with peppy steps on their way to celebrate a private Mass. All exuded excitement over their pilgrimage together.

The line of vans at the airport to transport pilgrims to Lourdes, with not a sedan in sight, attests to the Church's wisdom that we are made for community. We need other believers on our faith walk, yet I had come spiritually alone.

Of course, it is OK to go on a pilgrimage alone. In fact, my natural tendency is to do things alone. Many times I'm presented with the lesson, though, that there are times to fight against our natural ways. What's

2   "Miraculous healings," Lourdes Sanctuaire, https://www.lourdes-france.com/en/miraculous-healings/.

important is to examine our inclinations. Discerning the difference between embracing our tendencies or standing up to them is inner work that yields to the Holy Spirit.

Although I didn't experience the pilgrimage I desired, I'm grateful for the pilgrimage God gave me. I returned a strengthened believer, reminded that a missionary heart goes to the beloved, not the other way around. Our thirst drives us to other shores to quench, even if partially, a loved one's *no*. And there are times to square off, toe-to-toe, with our natural tendencies, and wrestle against them for virtue, for truth.

Finally, Our Lady has fortified this vessel with St. Paul's consoling words on behalf of her loved ones: Love (maybe even foolish love) never fails (1 Corinthians 13:8).

Blessed are those who have not lost hope (Sirach 14:2).

Frances Smit serves in-the-pews Catholics seeking more by sharing stories that hold spaces for encounters with God. Whether penning witness stories, writing children's books, or catechizing littles, she invites others to experience God's love through story. Because with God, there's always more. Read more *fbsmit.substack.com*

XXVII

MOTHER OF HOPE

How Mary Grieves with Us and Teaches
Us to Fix Our Eyes on Heaven

Lisa Rae Suppon

We are not orphans: We have a Mother
in heaven . . . she is the Mother of Hope.[1]

—Pope Francis

When Pope Francis announced 2025 as a Jubilee year, he invited the whole Church on a pilgrimage of hope. But if I am being honest, hope scares me.

Inherently a vulnerable act, hope puts you in touch with your deep longing and the desires that drive it, aware of the emptiness but moving forward with open hands in a sense of anticipation that it will be filled. When things that are hoped for instead return disappointment, we can be left disoriented and confused. Even when we experience the joy of our hopes being fulfilled, due to the transience of life, all good things eventually come to an end—sometimes tragically. To let ourselves be

---

1   Pope Francis, General Audience, May 10, 2017, https://www.vatican.va/content/francesco/en/audiences/2017/documents/papa-francesco_20170510_udienza-generale.html.

shaped and formed by what hope is on this side of Eden, we can't talk about hope without talking about grief. And the courage to grieve is the ultimate act of hope, because you are reaching out and risking the hope that a love larger than your pain will reach back.

Trauma expert Dr. Gabor Maté explains that "trauma is not what happens to us, but what we hold inside in the absence of an empathetic witness.[2]" Essentially, our pain stays with us if we don't have support from others. Imagine a small child learning to ride a bike for the first time. If she falls, her fear and pain kick in, and she cries out for someone. If her mother rushes in to hold her, comfort her, and attune to her pain, the girl will feel safe enough to fall apart and process her experience. She will learn that yes, the world can be a dangerous place. But she will also learn in her body that when scary things happen, she will be OK because a bigger love will come rushing in to find her. If, instead, no one comes, she won't feel safe enough to process that fear, and alone, she will become more anxious and hypervigilant.[3] Anxiety is "orphaned fear" that hasn't found its way home.

If we want to learn how to engage our grief to hope well, we simply can't do it alone. We need a bigger love that comes rushing in. Pope Francis also knew this, and that's why, in 2020, in the midst of global unrest and hopelessness, he added the title "Mother of Hope" to the Litany of Loreto.[4] To be pilgrims of hope, we need a mom!

In the first year of our marriage, my husband and I faced difficulty conceiving. We scheduled an appointment with a local Catholic fertility doctor for answers. But before the appointment, something in me urged

---

2   Peter A. Levine, *In An Unspoken Voice: How the Body Reveals Trauma and Restores Goodness* (Berkeley, CA: North Atlantic Books, 2010), xii.

3   This is my own paraphrasing of a concept I was taught by psychologist Dr. Tori Olds, in a course teaching about the nervous system, trauma, and resource. "Ethical Trauma Treatment," https://toriolds.com/ethical-trauma-treatment-understanding-the-needs-of-the-nervous-system/.

4   Vatican News, "Pope adds three new invocations to the Litany of the Blessed Virgin Mary," VaticanNews, June 20, 2020, https://www.vaticannews.va/en/pope/news/2020-06-pope-francis-loreto-litany-new-invocations.html.

us to stop. "Let's make a pilgrimage first," I said to my husband. In the uncertainty of what lay ahead, we both agreed it would be healing to connect with what was certain: we could trust that Mary would bring our hearts' intentions more perfectly to Jesus. So before we went to a doctor, we went to Africa.

In 1981, Mary began appearing in the poor hills of Kibeho, Rwanda. To date, these are the only Vatican-approved apparitions in Africa. I always felt a special connection here, as my own mother was carrying me in her womb at the time. Coming as a mother moved by her love not only for Rwanda but for the whole world, Mary was grieved by the hatred, division, and unforgiveness among her children, and urgently made a plea for people to return to God. She prophetically warned—with vivid images—that death would come to Rwanda if people didn't heed the message.[5] Tragically, the genocide she foretold did come to pass in 1994. Our little pilgrimage group was led by a woman who survived this tragedy, author and inspiring speaker Immaculée Ilibagiza. As a personal witness to some of the public apparitions, the tragedy that unfolded, and the miraculous reconciliation of her people, her eyes and her words made Our Lady's presence tangible in Kibeho.

What struck me most about what we learned there was that even though there was a sense of urgency in the warnings and the missions given to the visionaries, Mary first spent significant time communicating herself as a tender-hearted mother. For example, during her apparitions to the first visionary, Alphonsine, they would talk about her grades, what was going on at school, her friendships, etc. Alphonsine spent much of the time dancing and singing songs that Mary would teach her.[6] Sometimes Mary even danced along! When the crowds gathered to witness the apparitions, even though they could only observe Alphonsine as if she was talking on the phone, she sounded just like a sweet kid speaking

---

5   Immaculée Ilibagiza, *Our Lady of Kibeho* (Carlsbad, CA: Hay House, 2008) 148–151.
6   Ibid., 78.

affectionately to her mom. When asked why she used such familiar terms, Alphonsine responded matter-of-factly, "Because she asked us to talk to her like she's our mom, not like she's our principal or boss."[7]

Touched by these stories, and the miracles that still occurred there, my husband and I sat like children on the red dirt of the Rwandan hills where Mary danced, and talking to her "like she's our mom," we left our intentions.

Five months after we returned, we went to see the doctor, and after only the initial tests, we were told it would not just be difficult, it would be impossible for us to have children. As the room seemed to close in on me, all I could see was our doctor's face in genuine pain, and I was comforted knowing it hurt her so much to have to hurt us. I later learned that she waited almost two days after getting the results before calling us in so she could pray first. Our pain mattered and was held so mercifully.

Sometimes on this pilgrimage, we are going to walk straight into a dark night of the soul. Together, my husband and I had to learn to carry a profound longing that was beyond our power to fill, with an ache that would remain with us for the rest of our lives. I remember being disoriented by the fact that the rest of the world moved along so casually while everything for us had stopped. Even feeling offended by the sun at one point, I scoffed at the sky, "Don't you know that it's dark down here?" Needing some*thing* to attune to me, I painted my writing room black, ceiling included, and nestled there in my little cave. I wondered if maybe the dark night was an opportunity to know myself, God, and his mother in ways I hadn't yet known. Maybe darkness didn't have to be scary.

Maybe it was also a womb.

For years, I couldn't think about Rwanda or Our Lady of Kibeho. Eventually, I painfully had to admit to myself that I had tied my hope to a specific outcome. A part of me really believed I had fully surrendered my intentions there, but when a miracle didn't come as it did for others,

---

7 Ibid., 44.

I think my hope lay down and fell asleep right there in the red soil where we set it.

Even back home, as I tried to talk through things to begin making sense of the pain, I was often abruptly met with conversations about miracles, novenas, and scripture. "You just have to pray like Hannah!" I understand why people do this, I really do. On one hand, it's hard to look at another's pain, being vividly reminded of our own grief and that we aren't in heaven yet. And on the other hand, I know there is a genuine sense of compassion that moves people to try to rush through rationalizing things while offering a cheaply spiritualized version of hope, trying to rescue the hurting one from hopelessness. But here's the thing: the pain of grief isn't what drives a person to hopelessness. It's pain that is *alone*.

Providentially, Immaculée released another book during this time, which highlighted one crucial aspect of Mary's message to Rwanda that I had forgotten: a renewal of devotion to her seven sorrows.[8] I took this as an invitation to go back to Kibeho in my heart.

The mission of teaching the world the Seven Sorrows Rosary was assigned to the saucy, independent, and charismatic Marie Claire Mukangango. I remembered how much I loved this visionary, because when Mary first visited Marie Claire, calling out "Mukangango" in a tender, motherly voice that was "soothing as a lullaby," the born fighter responded with her fists high up in the air like a boxer. When Mary repeated her name, Marie Claire responded, "Okay, you've found me! I'm Munkangago, and I'm ready to fight!" Mary, ever a mother, was not offended but affectionately laughed, saying, "Why would you want to fight me, my child? What is making you so afraid? Never be afraid of your mother!"[9]

---

8   Immaculée Ilibagiza, *A Blessing in Disguise: Miracles of the Seven Sorrows Rosary* (Carlsbad, CA: Hay House, 2023).
9   Ibid., 16.

Mary also showed that she had a soft spot for Marie Claire, the girl with so much passion that she became the only one in recorded history to challenge her to a fistfight. Mary called her "The Cherished of the Blessed Mother." What is profound about this is that Marie Claire's father, who died when she was little, called her "Cherished of Daddy." Mary had intentionally adopted part of a familiar nickname to make the girl feel seen, known, and loved.[10]

Mary eventually showed Marie Claire a black rosary she had never seen before—the rosary of the Seven Sorrows—and taught her about each sorrow and the prayers associated with it. Even though she learned to recite the words by heart, Mary emphasized that to pray this devotion well, "you have to . . . put yourself in my place as you pray and ask yourself what I felt and what you would feel if it had been you." Marie Claire realized she had to be intentional in meditating on the sorrows that Jesus' mother experienced. As she put herself in Mary's shoes, more and more her heart broke. "Her sorrow commingled with Mary's . . . made her feel even more loved by and *closer* to Mary."[11]

I started to understand that Jesus and Mary don't share their sorrow with us to overwhelm us, or to avoid our pain, *but to connect*. To reach back.

After the apparitions, Marie Claire eventually went on to marry, and I learned also had to carry the cross of being childless. During the genocide, she was killed along with her husband.[12] It is a profound mystery that "The Cherished of the Blessed Mother" suffered this way, but I like to think that in her last moments, she once again saw the face of a mother whose love was bigger than her pain.

I set my book down and went to find my husband. "We did get our miracle in Kibeho! It wasn't a baby. It was *her*." And suddenly I could see the kindness of God in his providence, knowing the cross he would ask us

---

10 Ibid., 18.
11 Ibid., 148 (emphasis added).
12 Ibid., 24.

to carry together, had first called us to Kibeho, where we would find Mary as the perfect mother for our grief. And looking at my husband, I could also see the kindness of a God who, knowing the cross that was ahead for me, provided a partner who would pursue heaven wholeheartedly with me.

"We'll conceive hope," my husband says.

In the tenderness of this realization, it was as if Mary turned me around so I could finally see the face of the one who had been carrying me all along, teaching me to grieve not from a distance, but carried in her womb, so that I might hope again within my own.

"Never be afraid of your mother."

I walked over to my large white statue of Mary in my writing room, starkly contrasted against the night walls, and reached forward to trace the superimposed heart, trying to imagine all the sorrow she had shared with her Son, her pilgrim feet always in step with hope. This beautiful heart, not hidden from me, but given as a gift. And while touching hers, I placed my other hand on my own heart, rubbing the pain and mentally tracing the sorrow of my unwept tears. Now held by a bigger love, I let the tears fall.

I could hear a whisper deep inside responding, "I know, child. I know." And hope is already there, in a relationship.

Now, we come to the crowning moment of her role as Mother of Hope on our pilgrimage: she tenderly brings our hope to its final home: her Son.

Hope is not just a virtue we are learning to live out, but it is first and foremost a gift freely given to us by God (see CCC 1813). We are already being saved by the love the Holy Spirit bears witness to within us, a love from which we will never be separated. And as Pope Benedict says so profoundly in his encyclical *Spe Salvi* (Saved in Hope), we are not just left with conviction for emptiness that will be filled. But it is our faith that brings us the hoped-for "not yet" and gives us something of substance even now, as if "in embryo."[13]

And from this place, the whole Church may join our hearts with Elizabeth, another woman who knew the impossibility of her emptiness being filled, and together with her may we also say, "Why has this happened to me, that the mother of my lord comes to me?" (Luke 1:43). For at the sound of Mary's greeting, hope within us leaps for joy.

Heaven starts now.

Mother of our grief, Mother of hope, pray for us.

Lisa Rae Suppon, MT-BC, is a board-certified music therapist, with specialized training in hospice and palliative care music therapy. When not busy with her husband and three large poodles, she enjoys playing the piano, studying Theology of the Body, and learning about Internal Family Systems and parts work from a Catholic perspective. She focuses her writing around the intersection of faith, hope, grief, and music. See *instagram.com/lisaraesuppon*.

---

13 Pope Benedict XVI, *Spe Salvi*, November 30, 2007, sec. 7, https://www.vatican.va/content/benedict-xvi/en/encyclicals/documents/hf_ben-xvi_enc_20071130_spe-salvi.html.

XXVIII

Spiritual Vessel

How Mary Receives and Transmits God's Grace to Each of Us

Helen Syski

But we hold this treasure in earthen vessels, that the
surpassing power may be of God and not from us.

—2 Corinthians 4:7–10

The life-size silver crucifix was warmed by the candlelight as the priest's hands moved over the bread and wine during consecration. I shifted my weight from one knee to the other, struggling to keep awake. If only I could shift the weight in my eyelids . . .

High school's academic and athletic demands meant that Sunday Mass was the one moment of the week when my innards unwound their knot of tension. Without that knot's bulge propping my eyelids open, they dropped shut every time.

Why are you even here? Do you actually believe that bread and wine are really Jesus? The questions slithered through my mind. I jolted awake. The priest genuflected and then raised the Eucharist above his head. I watched him perform the rite I had seen every Sunday, suddenly aware in a new way. What did I believe was happening up there? Did I *really* know that Jesus was there?

In a flash I knew that I did not. Not the way I knew my parents loved me, that I would go to school tomorrow, and that I hated tomatoes. I had been told Jesus was there, that was all. I weighed the evidence. Everything else the Church told me about God made sense, and I certainly believed in a God powerful enough to transform bread into himself. So I would let him be powerful enough to take care of this too.

God, I will believe with my mind. It's up to you to make me know with my heart.

It would be a few years before he answered my prayer, and when he did it was through Mary under her title of Spiritual Vessel.

My freshman year at Harvard I took on leading the rosary prayer group. . . . and got tangled in some of the titles of the long Litany of Loreto recited at the end. Spiritual Vessel? Mystical Rose? The old creased and worn pamphlet obscured some of the letters, and in my ignorance "Tower of Ivory" became "Tower of Ivan."

One day a senior in the group looked down at me from his 6'7" heights and offered, "Hey, Helen, I'm reading the pope's encyclical on the Eucharist with some people. Are you interested?" I suspected a rebuke, but the kindness in his eyes suggested this was not an offer to reform me. He seemed to sense that I was open to learning more. With a start, I remembered the challenge I had thrown to God in high school. Perhaps, just maybe, he was taking me up on it.

"OK, sure."

The next weeks found our small group sitting on the burgundy cushioned chairs, the dim lamplight of the reception area the only sign of life left in the parish center at nine p.m. It was an interesting intellectual endeavor, but my heart was still not engaged. Then we reached the last chapter, "At the School of Mary," and we read:

> At the Annunciation Mary conceived the Son of God in the physical reality of his body and blood, thus anticipating within herself what to some degree happens sacramentally in every believer who receives, under the signs of bread and wine, the Lord's body and blood. . . .

When, at the Visitation, she bore in her womb the Word made flesh, she became in some way a "tabernacle"—the first "tabernacle" in history—in which the Son of God, still invisible to our human gaze allowed himself to be adored.[1]

My heart began to throb. Tabernacle . . . Mary . . . Spiritual Vessel . . . Awareness of the awesomeness of God become babe in Mary's womb lit up my heart. She carried God inside her, adoring him even before the world could see him. And this—this is what I get to do each Sunday when I receive him in the Eucharist. All I could hear was my own blood in my ears as the group moved on in their discussion. Pulse, life: Jesus' heart had beat as he grew inside his mama. Her blood, too, had pulsed and circulated, growing his divine little body.

I was barely conscious of everyone leaving and trekking back to their dorm rooms. I knew I too needed Mary. When praying for God to send grace to others through me, I would get an image in my mind of God pouring His grace through me, but the clay pot of my soul had too many cracks and chinks to hold it for long. Now I knew what to do. In my mind I placed my clay pot inside her perfect, whole vessel, already full of grace. Now her grace sealed my cracks, and I too could be full of grace to carry to the world.

"Spiritual Vessel" is one of the titles given to Mary by the Litany of Loreto. Composed during the Middle Ages, the litany was prayed at the Holy House of Loreto in Italy.[2] When all other Marian litanies were suppressed, this one was approved by Pope Sixtus V in 1587.[3]

---

1   St. John Paul II, *Ecclesia de Eucharistia*, 55.
2   According to tradition, the holy house of Loreto is the house from Nazareth where Mary received her Annunciation. The house is said to have been flown by angels from Palestine to the small town of Loreto in Italy in 1291. See H. Thurston, "Santa Casa di Loreto," in *The Catholic Encyclopedia* (New York: Robert Appleton Company), https://www.newadvent.org/cathen/13454b.htm.
3   "Litany of the Blessed Virgin Mary," EWTN, https://www.ewtn.com/catholicism/devotions/litany-of-loreto-246.

Spiritual means that something "ha[s] the nature of a spirit," but also that it is "of, from, or pertaining to God."[4] The word *spirit* comes from the Latin *spiritus*, meaning breath or breath of God.[5] Mary had not only her own spirit, her own breath of God of her own soul, but the Holy Spirit also dwelled within her, forming within her God himself in the flesh. She is both spiritual and Spiritual.

The word *vessel* can be used for many different things, perhaps most commonly "a hollow utensil used as a container, especially for liquids."[6] A container for liquids must be constructed with great care, because water is infamous for finding any weakness in a structure. Mary, who is "full of grace" (Luke 1:28), is a vessel that is perfectly constructed, able to hold the spiritual water of God's grace.

A vessel is not merely something used as a container, but can also be "a duct, canal, or other tube for containing or circulating a bodily fluid."[7] This meaning of the word also applies to Mary, who not only received Jesus in her heart and womb, but brought him forth to all of us. She is always bringing him to us, telling us as she told the servants at Cana, "Do whatever He tells you" (John 2:5).

Mary as Spiritual Vessel is not in danger of becoming stagnant or isolated. She is deeply connected to each of us, ready to birth Jesus into our hearts just as she gave him to the world. And like the wine at Cana, Jesus transforms our water not to alleviate our own thirst, but to refresh those he has placed in our lives.

The vessels in our bodies not only contain and circulate fluids, but they also absorb and release nutrients, clearing our systems of waste and toxins while delivering the food and resources needed for life. Similarly,

---

4 "Spiritual," *The American Heritage Dictionary of the English Language: New College Edition* (Boston: Houghton Mifflin Company, 1976).

5 "Spirit," *The American Heritage Dictionary of the English Language.*

6 "Vessel," Ibid.

7 Ibid.

Mary is channeling God's lifeblood throughout the Church and each of our hearts. She is cleansing as well as nourishing our souls.

The word *vessel* can also refer to "a craft, especially one larger than a rowboat, designed to navigate on water."[8] Mary was the vessel that carried Jesus into this life and through it, faithfully responding to the Father's hand at the tiller, keeping her sails filled with the Holy Spirit. In the seas of our life, as we journey as pilgrims, Mary is our vessel for a safe crossing, blown home by the breath of God.

This new understanding of Mary as Spiritual Vessel allowed the truth of the Eucharist to slide into my heart. The awesomeness of the truth could delight me rather than overwhelm me inside her snug hug.

The next Sunday as I approached the altar at Mass, I asked Mary to hold me, to capture the grace I was about to receive in the Eucharist, and allow me to steep in it for all time. And then once my cracks were healed, to open me, that I may not be merely a deposit of grace, but a conduit of God's lifeblood to others.

I felt more whole than I had ever felt before, and once again the knots inside me unwound. This time, though, the absence of the knots did not result in collapse. Instead, through Mary's intercession those unknotted vessels filled with grace, thrumming with His Life for the world.

Helen Syski is amazed by the adventures to be had in the wilds of God. A life-long New Englander and Harvard grad, Helen enjoys all four seasons and apple pie with her husband, children, and dogs. She is co-founder of the Kiss of Mercy Apostolate, a Little Way to heal the world from abortion. Continue the conversation at *AdequateAnthropologist.com*.

---

8   Ibid.

XXIX

MOTHER OF GOD

How Mary Teaches Us to Trust God

Veronica Vega

For the Mighty One has done great things for me.

—Luke 1:49

When I introduce myself to others, I may offer my first name, first and last name, job title, and even add other titles, descriptions, and accomplishments. Before I became a mom, most of my introductions focused primarily on me and my accomplishments. Adding the title of "Mom" changed everything. Throughout my children's school years, rarely would I introduce myself saying, "Hi, I'm Veronica." Instead, I became accustomed to introducing myself by saying, "Hi, I'm Joey's mom," or "Hi, I'm Vanessa's mom." That was a true lesson of joy and humility.

Now imagine the Blessed Virgin Mary stepping into our modern world and introducing herself. She has so many beautiful titles rich in meaning, but how about being known as the *Mother of God*? That is one powerful title. And what if she added more information? Of course, it would focus on her Son. "Hi, I'm Mary, the Mother of God. My Son is the Savior of the World." The reactions to her introduction would vary from awe and wonder to indifference and even disbelief.

Let's take it a step further. What if she were asked to present her resume? Reducing her accomplishments to a single page would not do her justice. Yet, in her humility, I think the only resume she would offer is the one we read in the Gospel of Luke: the Magnificat. In this sacred song, she reflects on her intimate relationship with both the Father and the Son, and it is clear she views this as the only accomplishment worth mentioning. Here is the beginning of that passage:

> And Mary said:
> "My soul magnifies the Lord;
> and my spirit rejoices in God my Savior,
> for he has looked with favor on the lowliness of his servant.
> Surely, from now on all generations will call me blessed;
> for the Mighty One has done great things for me,
> and holy is his name." (Luke 1:46–49)

We can learn much about Mary by looking to the Church, which teaches as dogma that Mary is truly the Mother of God. A dogma is a divinely revealed truth, taught by the Catholic Church, that must be believed by all the faithful. When it comes to Mary, we read in the *Catechism*: "What the Catholic faith believes about Mary is based on what it believes about Christ, and what it teaches about Mary illumines in turn its faith in Christ" (487).

The Gospels call Mary the mother of Jesus. Even before Jesus' birth, Mary's cousin Elizabeth greets the newly pregnant Mary as "the mother of my Lord" (Luke 1:43). Since Jesus is the Son of God and the second Person of the Blessed Trinity (see CCC 495), "the Council of Ephesus proclaimed in 431 that Mary truly became the Mother of God by the human conception of the Son of God in her womb" (CCC 466). The entire Church holds to this teaching and confesses this title. Mary is truly *Theotokos*, a Greek word meaning "God-bearer."

Moreover, "because of Mary's singular cooperation with the action of the Holy Spirit, the Church loves to pray, in communion with the Virgin Mary, to magnify with her the great things the Lord has done for her, and to entrust supplications and praises to her" (CCC 2682). In our lives as Catholics, we celebrate Mary as Mother of God on January 1, the eighth day of the Nativity of the Lord. On this holy day of obligation, the Church affirms Mary's role in salvation history and proclaims Jesus as fully human and fully divine.

We also invoke Mary as Mother of God in the principal Eucharistic prayers used in the Holy Sacrifice of the Mass:[1]

> **I:** In communion with those whose memory we venerate, especially the glorious ever-Virgin Mary, *Mother of our God* and Lord, Jesus Christ . . .
> **II:** Have mercy on us all, we pray, that with the blessed Virgin Mary, *Mother of God* . . .
> **III:** May he make of us an eternal offering to you, so that we may obtain an inheritance with your elect, especially with the most blessed Virgin Mary, *Mother of God* . . .
> **IV:** O merciful Father, that we may enter into a heavenly inheritance with the blessed Virgin Mary, *Mother of God* . . .

And we honor Mary with this title whenever we pray the Hail Mary. Along with the Lord's prayer, the Hail Mary is one of the most widely used prayers in the Catholic Church. The origin of the first half of the prayer is from the Annunciation in Luke's Gospel, and the second half is an intercessory prayer that comes from the Church's tradition.[2] It is in the second half of the Hail Mary that we invoke her under this title, when we pray, "Holy Mary, *Mother of God*, pray for us sinners, now and at the hour of our death. Amen."

+ + +

Prior to baptizing my children, I clearly recall a priest at the baptismal preparation class saying that it was the parents' job to get their kids

---

1   *The Roman Missal* (New Jersey: Catholic Book Publishing Corp., 2021).
2   *United States Catholic Catechism for Adults* (Washington, DC: United Conference of Catholic BIshops, 2012), 470–471.

to heaven. That moment marked the beginning of my mission, and I embraced it wholeheartedly. I made sure my little ones received their sacraments, learned their prayers, and attended the Holy Sacrifice of the Mass every Sunday and on holy days of obligation, come rain, shine, or vacation. Check, check, and check.

Although my understanding of the Bible and Rosary was limited at that time, I still searched for meaningful Bible passages to share with my children, and I did my best to pray the Rosary in part or in full as often as possible. Check and check again. I was committed to doing all I could to get my children to heaven.

When they graduated from high school, my role changed, but somehow I *missed the memo.* Or perhaps I ignored it because I was too focused on the mission. I tried everything to lead, but looking back, I see how much I micromanaged their spiritual journey. It took years, many more than I would like to admit, for me to realize that while I could lay the groundwork, the choice to be in relationship with God and to live out the Catholic faith was theirs alone. As Sirach 15:14 reminds us, "It was he who created humankind in the beginning, and he left them in the power of their own free choice."

Through it all, the Rosary remained the anchor of my prayer life. During this time, I fervently prayed for my children, fasted for them, and lifted them up every time I attended the Holy Sacrifice of the Mass. I know these acts were all very good and important to do. Yet, despite these acts and my growing understanding of Sacred Scripture and the Catholic faith, fear and worry continued to occupy my heart. The truth? I didn't fully trust God in the very depths of my soul. But God was carefully orchestrating his plan.

On the evening of February 24, 2021, after a long, exhausting day at work, I sat upon my bed, not wanting to do one more thing. Still, something prompted me—I believe it was the Holy Spirit. I remembered that the third day of a Lenten mission was scheduled at my parish, only two miles away. I genuinely wanted to attend, but didn't have the energy to drive even two miles. Thankfully, I remembered the mission was going to be livestreamed. I decided to watch and listen from the comfort of my bed.

The guest presenter was Fr. Philip Scott, whose words convey a deep and sincere love for the Father, Son, and Holy Spirit, as well as for the Blessed Mother, and their limitless love for us. About seventy minutes into his presentation, he mentioned something about children being away from the Church. Needless to say, my ears perked up, and I thought, "Maybe he'll share some words of wisdom to help me with my own kids."

He said, "I want you to give them to Jesus right now, through Mary." He continued, "I want you to give her—*name that situation, that person or people in your life that are away from the Church, or that situation that will not change.* Give it to her, and she is taking it, and she is putting it in her heart. Ask her to teach you to abandon that into the hands of God through her intercession."

Then he led us in prayer: "You promised, Jesus, that you would create a new heaven and a new earth. I want you to create a new person, people, situations." He prompted us, "Keep giving them to him almost to the point that they are more God's than yours.... Do not carry it anymore.... If we've lost our peace and our joy over this situation or this child that needs to be converted, then guess what, it has become bigger than God, which is not true." He continued in prayer, "Do not allow me, Jesus, to lose my peace and joy over these members of my family. You are taking care of them. You are working all day, all night, at 100 percent of your divinity, for their salvation. I ask you, Lord Jesus, to have the last word."

In that moment, something shifted inside of me. I knew exactly what I needed to do: let them go. My fear was at its pinnacle. I wept uncontrollably with deep, sorrowful tears into my pillow for what seemed like an hour. They weren't tears of joy, but rather of sadness upon the realization that I had been standing in the way of my children's journey to the Father, Son, and Holy Spirit.

Finally, when the tears subsided, an overwhelming peace filled my entire being. I knew from the very depths of my heart that Jesus loved my children more than I ever could, that he would take care of them, and that I could entrust them to Mary, the Mother of God, and ask her to give them to her Son.

I said out loud to the Blessed Mother, "I give you Joey and Vanessa to take to your Son." The weight of worry, fear, and sorrow lifted. That evening was transformational. From there, my prayers for my son and daughter no longer came from anxiety or desperation, but from genuine faith, hope, and love. The fruit from that surrender has been truly remarkable, as the Heavenly Father continues beautiful work in both their journeys.

Mary, the Mother of God, ceaselessly intercedes for us with her Son. Because of her gentleness, I received the grace to entrust my children to her, asking her to hold them in her most Immaculate Heart and give them to her Son, Jesus Christ. If that wasn't enough, her ongoing and most powerful intercession, especially through the Most Holy Rosary and by the power of the Holy Spirit, led me to a deeper and more intimate level of trust and faith in the mercy of her Son, not just for myself, but for others as well. Still, that wasn't the end.

Mary's unwavering example of surrender, obedience, and humility to the Father, not just at the Annunciation but throughout her life, opened the door to heal a profound wound of emptiness, sadness, and fear in my life since the loss of my earthly father, which I experienced at the age of seventeen. Over the years, the sadness lessened, but the emptiness and fear remained. I yearned for "my daddy," but by God's grace, I was gently drawn into the loving embrace of the Father and came to know myself as his beloved daughter. Though I will always miss "my daddy," the comfort and love our heavenly Father gives sustain and fulfill me each and every day.

Mary's resume is impressive, and her list of titles is numerous and beautiful. I humbly pray that, by God's mercy, I may one day be in heaven with Our Lord and Savior Jesus Christ, and that he will allow me to meet the Blessed Mother. On that day, I know she will need no introduction because my heart will immediately recognize her as Mary, *Mother of God.* If I'm able to speak, I will say, "Hi, Blessed Mother, I'm Veronica, beloved daughter of the Most High God. I love you and thank you for your *yes* to bringing forth the Savior of the world; for leading me closer to the Father, Son, and Holy Spirit; for showing me the beauty of motherhood, faith, trust, obedience, suffering, humility, and love; and for your ceaseless and powerful intercessions for me, for those I love, and for the world."

My prayer for you is that you will recognize how our Heavenly Father is drawing near to you in every moment, calling you to be an heir of his blessed life (see CCC 1), and that Mary, the Mother of God, will intercede for you according to her Son's perfect will.

Veronica Vega is a beloved daughter of the Most High God. Her mission is to help others learn how to deepen their personal, intimate relationship with the Father, Son, and Holy Spirit, accomplished through the lens of Sacred Scripture and the treasure of the Catholic Faith. She teaches OCIA classes and parish workshops, leads retreats, and is the founder of Open My Heart Lord Ministries. Learn more at her YouTube channel *youtube.com/@openmyheartlord2022.*

XXX

OUR LADY OF GUADALUPE

Crowned with the Glory of the Sun

Jeanne Dandrow

A great portent appeared in heaven:
a woman *clothed with the sun ...*

—Revelation 12:1

The sound of my footsteps echoed through the silent hallways as I searched for my room at the retreat center. I hated to admit it, but I was lost—both figuratively and literally. This was my first retreat, and my mind was too preoccupied with the fact that I was pregnant with our first child for me to focus on where I was going.

This baby in my womb was a miracle, something I had been told would be impossible. Now that my prayer had been answered, I wondered if I truly had what it takes to embrace this sacred call.

Grateful yet anxious, I scanned the hallways in search of my room. When I finally found it, I noticed that over the doorway there was a plaque with a title of Mary that I had never heard of: Our Lady of Guadalupe.

Still, at the sight of Our Lady's name, my heart was filled with a sense of peace, as though Mary had come to visit me. Happy to be in a space blessed and protected under her mantle, I also sensed a personal invitation to come to know her more deeply under this title.

Almost forty years later, I am still learning, as is much of the world.

The history of Our Lady of Guadalupe began in Mexico in December 1531, a decade after the Spanish conquest, when the Virgin Mary visited a newly baptized Indigenous man named Juan Diego.[1] She appeared as an expectant mother.

Introducing herself as the Ever-Virgin Mary, Mother of the True God, she called Juan Diego her "dearest little son" and gave him a mission: to ask the bishop to build her "a little house" (church) where, through her intercession, souls would find refuge in their sufferings. Our Lady promised him she would hear their weeping and heal their sorrows through her compassionate and merciful gaze.[2]

At first, Juan Diego was unable to convince the bishop that he had witnessed an apparition, and like many of us who struggle with self-doubt, he felt unworthy of his call. Mary then appeared to him again with a message that resonates with all of us who have been called to a task we feel is too difficult, or who need a reminder that we all have a mission only we are called to fulfill:

> Listen, my youngest and dearest son, know for sure that I have no lack of servants, of messengers, to whom I can give the task of carrying my breath, my word, so that they carry out my will; but it is very necessary that you, personally, go and plead, that my wish, my will become a reality, be carried out through your intercession.[3]

Encouraged by Mary's reassurance, Juan Diego did not give up. He courageously met with the bishop, who asked for a sign. In the next

---

1 Grzegorz Górny and Janusz Rosikon, *Guadalupe Mysteries: Deciphering the Code* (Ignatius Press, 2016),12–15
2 Antonio Valeriano, *Nican Mopohua,* in *Huei Tlamahuiçoltica* (1649). Translated as *Nican Mopohua: Here It Is Told (*Dominican Sisters of Springfield, 2009), 3–4.
3 Ibid., 6.

apparition, Mary promised to provide a sign when Juan Diego returned to her the next day. The following day, however, Juan Diego's uncle fell gravely ill. In the hopes of finding a priest for his uncle, Juan Diego felt he had no choice but to avoid meeting Mary at the apparition site.

Knowing his needs, Our Lady kindly intercepted him on the way, simultaneously appearing to his uncle, who was healed of his grave illness. She spoke these comforting and famous words to the now St. Juan Diego: "Let nothing worry you. . . Am I not here, I who am your mother? . . . Are you not in the crossing of my arms? Do you need something more?"[4]

Our Lady then instructed Juan to go to the top of Tepeyac Hill, to pick some flowers, and to bring them to her. Reaching the top of the hill, he stood in wonder as he beheld various flowers, including Castilian roses, which did not grow that time of year. In awe, he gathered them and took them to Mary, who arranged them in his tilma (cloak) to bring to the bishop.

Once in the bishop's presence, Juan Diego opened his tilma to present the flowers. They fell to the ground, revealing a miraculous image of the Blessed Mother. In their amazement, those present, including the bishop, fell to their knees.[5]

The image is now known as Our Lady of Guadalupe and is enshrined in the Basilica of Our Lady of Guadalupe in Mexico City, Mexico.

The beauty of the miraculous image of Our Lady of Guadalupe is in both its simplicity and symbolism. It is a sacred icon whose mysterious codes and properties have filled books and confounded scientists for centuries.

On the Tilma, Mary is depicted as a virgin maiden with both Indigenous and European features. Standing on the moon, she is dressed in a blue-green mantle covered with stars that inexplicably mirror the constellations visible from heaven on the day of the apparition.[6]

---

4   Ibid., 9–10.
5   Ibid., 13.
6   Górny and Rosikon, *Guadalupe Mysteries*, 55–64.

As if crowned with its glory, Mary is surrounded by the sun, with its rays radiating behind her. This was relevant because the posture and positioning of Mary on the tilma in front of the sun indicated to the Indigenous people that she was a queen who served the God who was greater than the gods the Aztecs worshiped, especially the sun god.

Wearing a black sash around her waist signifying pregnancy, and with a cross resting at her neck, her hands are folded in prayer.

Her eyes, which humbly gaze down upon her children with gentleness and compassion, have attracted the attention of devout souls for nearly 500 years. More recently, photographers and ophthalmologists have used many methods, including digital imaging, to study enlarged photographs of the image's eyes. In doing so, they discovered that they held a supernatural secret that would become a gift for future generations. Remarkably, when magnified, they revealed images of people reflected in them, as one would expect to see in a living eye. Specifically, mirrored in her eyes were Juan Diego, the bishop, and thirteen other people present who saw the image miraculously appear on Juan's tilma.[7]

These discoveries point to the truth that the message of Our Lady of Guadalupe was not only intended for the people of the sixteenth century but also for us today.

Her message from heaven came at a time when the indigenous people of Mexico, like much of our world today, were suffering greatly from the traumas of war, cultural divisions, disease, and a culture that embraced making human sacrifices to their gods. Through the colonization of the time, the indigenous people were losing their sense of identity, and the prophecies of their gods indicated that the end of the world was near.[8]

Does this sound familiar? At the time of this writing, we live in a war-torn world suffering from political divisions, disease, and violence. Ours is a culture that was described by St. John Paul II as "a culture of

---

7   Ibid., 233–247.
8   Ibid., 16–18

death" that disregards the sanctity of life and our dignity as children of God. Like the world in St. Juan Diego's time, our world today is also in want of hope and restoration. Of all the generations called to experience the power of venerating the Virgin of Guadalupe, perhaps ours is the one that is most in need of her motherly protection and powerful intercession.

She is known as the Patroness of Life because she is credited with ending the practice of child sacrifice among the Indigenous people of Mexico.[9] Her appearance not only united the Indigenous people of Mexico and their European colonizers but also, in just six years, led to the conversion of an estimated nine million souls to Catholicism in the Americas.[10]

Thus John Paul II declared Our Lady of Guadalupe Patroness of all America and Star of the first and new evangelization.[11] Her message and the image she left us give us great hope in the midst of turbulent times.

+ + +

Looking back at that first day on the retreat, I realize that Our Lady of Guadalupe was offering me hope when I needed it most. Knowing that she is the Patroness of life gave me hope my pregnancy would be fine, and when I won a blue rosary in a raffle, I felt comforted by her presence. At the time, I wondered if the color was a sign that we would have a boy.

My husband and I would find out the answer sooner than expected when, a few months later, at twenty-four weeks of pregnancy, I was rushed to the hospital, clutching those beads in my hands. The hospital confirmed what I already knew: I was in premature labor. My baby was in danger of death.

Clinging to my rosary in prayer, fearing I would never be able to hold my child in my arms, I asked Mary to hold him in hers. We prayed for

---

9 Górny and Rosikon, *Guadalupe Mysteries*, 194.

10 Ibid., 48.

11 John Paul II, *Ecclesia in America*, 1999, https://www.vatican.va/content/john-paul-ii/en/apost_exhortations/documents/hf_jp-ii_exh_22011999_ecclesia-in-america.html.

a miracle. Our community prayed for us as well, and once the doctors stabilized me, I was ordered to go home for three months of bed rest. During this time, I found refuge in Our Lady through the habit of praying the Rosary every day.

Thankfully, our prayers were answered, and we brought our little butterball, Jonathan, home during Thanksgiving week.

When Our Lady of Guadalupe appeared to St. Juan Diego, she called him her "dearest little son." At times, when I held our "dearest little son" in my arms, our eyes would meet in a loving gaze, and in those precious moments between mother and child, I realized he did not have to do or be anything special to earn my love.

He needed, trusted, and depended on me for everything because he was too little to do anything on his own, and as his parents, we would do or sacrifice anything for him. This image of mother and child mirrors God's relationship with us.

No matter how little or powerless we feel when facing the harsh realities of this world, we are all seen, known, and loved by God as his beloved children, and he will always take care of us. He has solidarity with us because he shares in our sufferings, and he desires for us to share in his glory. These are some of the greatest messages of Our Lady of Guadalupe.

Contemplating the image of Our Lady of Guadalupe helps us enter into these mysteries of God's unconditional love for us, and so I invite you to prayerfully sit before her image and behold the loving gaze of your heavenly mother, Our Lady of Guadalupe. Her image can be found in multiple places online, including kofc6693.org/our-lady-of-guadalupe. Mary promised St. Juan Diego that, with her compassionate gaze, she will manifest our Lord, heal our hearts, and aid in our salvation.[12] Knowing this, as you receive her gaze, ask her with confidence to help you to see in her eyes a reflection of God's unconditional love for you.

---

12 Valeriano, *Nican Mopohua*, 3–4, 10.

As you meditate on her image, recall these words she spoke to Juan as though they are being spoken to you, because they are:

"Let nothing worry you. . . Am I not here, I who am your mother? . . . Are you not in the crossing of my arms? Do you need something more?"

We can rest assured that when we behold the eyes of our heavenly mother pictured in the image of Our Lady of Guadalupe, heaven beholds us.

Oh beautiful, tender Mother, Our Lady of Guadalupe, crowned with the glory of your Son, pray for us so that we may be clothed with your virtue and share in his glory. Amen.

Jeanne Dandrow is a beloved child of God, wife, mother, retired teacher, and a Lay Dominican. Her witness stories and meditations can be found in the book, *Godhead Here in Hiding, Whom I do Adore*, compiled by the Lay Dominicans and Fr Ignatius Schweitzer, O.P.

XXXI

OUR LADY UNDOER OF KNOTS

How Mary's Maternal Love Sees Us Through Everything

Katherine Blakeman

*On the third day there was a wedding in Cana of Galilee,
and the mother of Jesus was there. Jesus and his disciples
had also been invited to the wedding. When the wine
gave out, the mother of Jesus said to him, "They have no
wine." And Jesus said to her, "Woman, what concern is
that to you and to me? My hour has not yet come." His
mother said to the servants, "Do whatever he tells you."*

—John 2: 1–5

"Mama! Would you please get this knot out of my doll's hair?" I can sense the frustration in both of my little girls' voices when one of their doll's hair is knotted and they can't untangle it. I can hear the desperation in my three-year-old son's voice if the drawstring on his pants is in a knot and he needs to use the restroom. "Mama, I need to go potty, and I can't untie this! Please help me!"

As a mother of four small children, I am no stranger to pressing pleas for help, particularly when my little ones cannot help themselves or have already tried to no avail. *Merriam-Webster* defines *frustration* as "a deep chronic sense or state of insecurity and dissatisfaction arising from unresolved problems or unfulfilled needs."[1] If those needs remain unfulfilled long enough, or they are very acute, we can reach a state of *desperation*, or a "loss of hope and surrender to despair."[2]

Haven't we all felt that way in the face of some seemingly intractable problem or crisis? And are we not all little children in the eyes of our eternal God?

Our sin and ignorance often leave us in a state of frustrated desperation, especially in the sphere of our horizontal, human relationships. Like a toddler with a plate of spaghetti on our tray, we can really make a mess of things.

Thankfully, in his infinite wisdom, our Heavenly Father has given us a mother unparalleled in patience and surpassing all mankind in wisdom. Her supremely loving heart and nimble fingers are ever ready and willing to untangle our knots. She eagerly listens as we beseech her for help. She guides us through the twists and turns in our strained relationships and helps disentangle us from sin and vice.

With finesse, our Blessed Mother replaces frustration with peace. She dispels despair and restores hope. The peace of Christ is the answer to all our entanglements and enmeshments; Our Lady is the dispenser of that peace. Our part is simply to come to her as humble little children and ask for her help.

And on the absolute necessity of being childlike, our Lord Jesus was very clear. "Truly I tell you, unless you change and become like children, you will never enter the kingdom of heaven" (Matthew 18:3). What all little children have in common is their utter dependency upon their parents for, well, everything! Dependency is so humbling. It's a constant reminder that we are nothing and can do nothing without God's divine grace, the Mediatrix of which is our loving mother Mary.

---

1   "Frustration," *Merriam-Webster*, https://www.merriam-webster.com/dictionary/frustration.

2   "Desperation," *Merriam-Webster*, https://www.merriam-webster.com/dictionary/desperation.

It is precisely as little children, then, humbled by our own weakness and inadequacy to resolve our various problems, that we can call upon our heavenly mother under her title Our Lady Undoer of Knots. In our moments of desperation, especially when we are suffering turmoil caused by knotted, twisted, or dysfunctional relationships, or when we feel tethered to a particular habitual sin, we are irresistible to our sweet Mother.

When we call upon Our Lady Undoer of Knots, she shows up in spectacular fashion. Father Chris Alar of the Marian Fathers of the Immaculate Conception testified to the sheer power of this devotion when he said, "Our Lady Undoer of the Knots I do not use often. She's a big gun I only bring out in times of crisis, but it has never failed me." He continued, "I have used her three times . . . and those three times were knots in my life that I did not think could ever be undone, and all three were."

In fact, one of the major knots in his life caused him to doubt his very vocation to the priesthood. After a sincere novena, or nine days of prayer, to Our Lady Undoer of Knots, this threat to his priesthood was totally and completely removed.[3]

Like Father Chris, I have turned to Our Lady under this powerful title when I was at some of my most challenging points in close relationships or struggling with unforgiveness of myself and others.

In one particular case, I asked for a specific sign as to how to proceed in a strained relationship: a red flower for one course of action, a white flower for the other. After a novena, I was given the sign I asked for. This sign directed me not to lose hope, but to keep asking for the humility and strength to resolve the issue. Following this novena, I knew I was not alone, relying on my own ineffective or perhaps misguided efforts to

---

3   Fr. Chris Alar, "Our Lady Undoer of Knots – Explaining the Faith w/ Fr. Chris Alar," Divine Mercy Channel, July 6, 2024, YouTube, 1:30, https://www.youtube.com/watch?v=gTgo1HfXI34.

restore peace and order in my life. Instead, I was able to journey forward in faith, disentangled from the fear which previously ensnared me.

Like a little child who is afraid to be alone in the dark, and who would likely only tighten the knots entangling me, I wanted to know my Blessed Mother was guiding me with her graceful hands, and through this devotion she gave me solace.

It is no surprise that another rocky relationship, a marriage on the verge of collapse, served as the springboard some four centuries ago for this now burgeoning devotion. Human nature was no less fallen in the year 1615, when German nobleman Wolfgang Langenmantel discovered his wife, Sofia, was planning to divorce him. In his distress, Langenmantel sought counsel from Fr. Jakob Rem, known for his devotion to Our Lady.

At the last of four meetings between the two men, Fr. Rem was presented with the troubled couple's wedding ribbon, which, according to the German custom of that time, was tied around the spouses hands at their wedding to symbolize their lifelong union. Fr. Rem raised the ribbon, untying its knots before an image of Our Lady of the Snows. Upon completion of his prayer for the couple, the ribbon became dazzlingly white. This small miracle represented the larger miraculous intercession at play, as Our Lady unraveled the knots in a broken marriage and restored its integrity.

Eighty-five years later the fortunate couple's grandson, Fr. Hieronymus Ambrosius Langenmantel, commissioned Johann Georg Melchior Schmidtner to paint an image of Our Lady dedicated to Our Lady of Good Counsel for an altar donated by the Langenmantel family to the church of St. Peter am Perlach. Inspired by the incredible story of Our Lady's intercession in the Langenmantels' marriage, the artist depicted Our Lady graciously untying knots in a long white ribbon.[4]

---

4   Mark Nelson, *Understanding Mary Undoer of Knots: How an obscure German painting became the world's fastest growing Marian devotion and is changing lives today* (Steubenville Press, 2013), 6–7.

The devotion remained almost exclusively in Germany and Europe for many years, until Pope Francis, then Jorge Bergolio, was studying for the priesthood in Germany in 1980. He fell in love with the painting of Our Lady Undoer of Knots and helped to spread the devotion to his native Argentina, and later, around the world.

Given the universality of our fallen nature and sinfulness, the popularity of this devotion is no surprise. Our common, primordial need for a good Mother to undo knots for us reaches back to the beginning of human history, when our first parents fell to Satan's temptation in the Garden of Eden, beginning with our first mother, Eve.

And our good, good God provided, when his beloved Son uttered some of the tenderest words ever spoken. As our Savior Jesus Christ gasped for his last breaths on the Cross, he said to his mother: "Woman, here is your son." Then he said to the beloved disciple, John, "Here is your mother" (John 19:26–27).

In his second-century work *Against Heresies,* St. Irenaeus first used the imagery of untying a knot to depict the contrast between Eve's disobedience and Mary's obedience. He wrote, "The knot of Eve's disobedience was loosed by the obedience of Mary. For what the virgin, Eve, had bound fast through unbelief, this did the virgin Mary set free through faith."

That perfect obedience—Mary's constant, unshakable unity with God's will—is precisely what makes her so uniquely qualified to untie our knots. While we have a great many wonderful intercessors in our friends, the saints, Our Lady alone was never once ensnared by even the smallest of sins against God or neighbor. Her immaculate purity and perfect humility make Mary our most powerful intercessor in heaven.

Devotion to Our Lady Undoer of Knots is spreading rapidly today, and for good reason. We see nations teetering on the edge of nuclear conflict, forgetful that Christ is King, and thus eschewing the grace and protection he offers societies. The wicked tentacles of pornography addiction seem to have tightened around the entire globe, fueled by the Internet. Assaults on marriage and the family are as never before imagined (though Our Lady of Fatima warned us). Young people suffer ever increasing levels of isolation in the age of social media (or as I prefer to call it, antisocial media), leaving many in a state of frazzled despair and loneliness.

Call upon Our Lady Undoer of Knots when the hatred and violence in our nation and world seem completely overwhelming, remembering that she and Jesus have the final victory.

Pray to Our Lady Undoer of Knots with the humility of a small child when you are in crisis, too. She never refuses to come to the aid of her children. She is the tenderest of mothers and an unparalleled intercessor, because she's irresistible to God. Just think of how she interceded with Jesus on behalf of a newlywed couple whose stomachs were probably in knots as they ran out of wine at their wedding feast. Think also of her unimaginable, motherly mercy, a luminous reflection of her Divine Son's unfathomable mercy, as she unhesitatingly took us on as her children, despite our sins nailing her Son to the Cross.

I would leave you with this. Call out to your heavenly mother under any title you wish. As you've journeyed through her titles in this book, you've encountered Our Lady from so many beautiful angles. Consider invoking her under this title during your most difficult or seemingly insurmountable relationship conflicts or battles with personal sin. There are many versions of the Our Lady Undoer of Knots novena, including a Rosary version, that are powerful. Find the prayer or novena you like best. Pray it. Then rest in her maternal arms.

May God bless you, and may our Blessed Mother wrap you tightly in her mantle as she unties the knots in the ribbon of your life.

Katherine Blakeman (née Rosario) is a graduate of Ave Maria University with a Bachelor of Arts in politics. She is a wife and homeschooling mother of four. She previously served as communications director for the National Center on Sexual Exploitation and for former Congressman Keith Rothfus and currently writes for Catholic Women in Business.

Official Act of Consecration to Mary

Written by St. Maximilian Kolbe

O IMMACULATA, Queen of Heaven and earth, refuge of sinners and our most loving Mother, God has willed to entrust the entire order of mercy to you. I, (name), a repentant sinner, cast myself at your feet humbly imploring you to take me with all that I am and have, wholly to yourself as your possession and property. Please make of me, of all my powers of soul and body, of my whole life, death and eternity, whatever most pleases you.

If it pleases you, use all that I am and have without reserve, wholly to accomplish what was said of you: "She will crush your head," and, "You alone have destroyed all heresies in the world." Let me be a fit instrument in your immaculate and merciful hands for introducing and increasing your glory to the maximum in all the many strayed and indifferent souls, and thus help extend as far as possible the blessed kingdom of the most Sacred Heart of Jesus. For wherever you enter, you obtain the grace of conversion and growth in holiness, since it is through your hands that all graces come to us from the most Sacred Heart of Jesus.

V. Allow me to praise you, O sacred Virgin.
R. Give me strength against your enemies

THE LITANY OF LORETO

Lord have mercy.	*Christ have mercy.*
Lord have mercy. Christ hear us.	*Christ graciously hear us.*
God, the Father of heaven,	*have mercy on us.*
God the Son, Redeemer of the world,	*have mercy on us.*
God the Holy Spirit,	*have mercy on us.*
Holy Trinity, one God,	*have mercy on us.*
Holy Mary,	*pray for us.*
Holy Mother of God,	*pray for us.*
Holy Virgin of virgins,	*pray for us.*
Mother of Christ,	*pray for us.*
Mother of the Church,	*pray for us.*
Mother of Mercy,	*pray for us.*
Mother of divine grace,	*pray for us.*
Mother of Hope,	*pray for us.*
Mother most pure,	*pray for us.*
Mother most chaste,	*pray for us.*
Mother inviolate,	*pray for us.*
Mother undefiled,	*pray for us.*
Mother most amiable,	*pray for us.*
Mother admirable,	*pray for us.*
Mother of good counsel,	*pray for us.*
Mother of our Creator,	*pray for us.*
Mother of our Saviour,	*pray for us.*
Virgin most prudent,	*pray for us.*
Virgin most venerable,	*pray for us.*
Virgin most renowned,	*pray for us.*
Virgin most powerful,	*pray for us.*
Virgin most merciful,	*pray for us.*
Virgin most faithful,	*pray for us.*
Mirror of justice,	*pray for us.*
Seat of wisdom,	*pray for us.*
Cause of our joy,	*pray for us.*
Spiritual vessel,	*pray for us.*
Vessel of honour,	*pray for us.*
Singular vessel of devotion,	*pray for us.*
Mystical rose,	*pray for us.*

Tower of David,	*pray for us.*
Tower of ivory,	*pray for us.*
House of gold,	*pray for us.*
Ark of the covenant,	*pray for us.*
Gate of heaven,	*pray for us.*
Morning star,	*pray for us.*
Health of the sick,	*pray for us.*
Refuge of sinners,	*pray for us.*
Solace of Migrants,	*pray for us.*
Comfort of the afflicted,	*pray for us.*
Help of Christians,	*pray for us.*
Queen of Angels,	*pray for us.*
Queen of Patriarchs,	*pray for us.*
Queen of Prophets,	*pray for us.*
Queen of Apostles,	*pray for us.*
Queen of Martyrs,	*pray for us.*
Queen of Confessors,	*pray for us.*
Queen of Virgins,	*pray for us.*
Queen of all Saints,	*pray for us.*
Queen conceived without original sin,	*pray for us.*
Queen assumed into heaven,	*pray for us.*
Queen of the most holy Rosary,	*pray for us.*
Queen of families,	*pray for us.*
Queen of peace.	*pray for us.*

Lamb of God, who takes away the sins of the world,	*spare us, O Lord.*
Lamb of God, who takes away the sins of the world,	*graciously hear us, O Lord.*
Lamb of God, who takes away the sins of the world,	*have mercy on us.*

Pray for us, O holy Mother of God.

That we may be made worthy of the promises of Christ.

Let us pray.

Grant, we beseech thee, O Lord God, that we, your servants, may enjoy perpetual health of mind and body; and by the glorious intercession of the Blessed Mary, ever Virgin, may be delivered from present sorrow, and obtain eternal joy. Through Christ our Lord. Amen.

CATHOLICITY · CREATIVITY · COMMUNITY

Join us today at

praisewriters.com